228 Interesting, Odd, Beautiful & Historic
THINGS TO SEE
IN SANTA CRUZ COUNTY

We welcome your comments and suggestions.

Santa Cruz County is an immensely interesting place. We want to make sure we keep this guide useful, accurate, and up-to-date, and we would appreciate any comments or suggestions that would help us improve future editions of this book.

Please send your comments to:

Editorial Department
Journeyworks Publishing
P.O. Box 8466
Santa Cruz, CA 95061-8466

Or email: editorial@journeyworks.com

Thanks!

228 Interesting, Odd, Beautiful & Historic THINGS TO SEE IN SANTA CRUZ COUNTY

Steven Bignell and Susan Bruijnes

Journeyworks Publishing • Santa Cruz, CA 95060

Graphic Design by Eva Bernstein and Su Gatch

Cover Design by Su Gatch

Photo Credits:

Christian Riblet page 121
Tim Matthews page 127
Stephan Bianchi page 114
Robert Ritchey page 221
Courtesy of Library of Congress pages 15, 178
All other photos by the authors.

ISBN 978-1-56885-752-7

Manufactured in the United States of America

Published by: Journeyworks Publishing
                   P.O. Box 8466
                   Santa Cruz, CA 95061-8466
                   www.journeyworks.com

An Important Caution to Our Readers

Readers must assume personal responsibility for their safety and security when visiting any of the sights described in this book and should exercise appropriate caution and common sense.

The authors and Journeyworks Publishing assume no liability for damage or loss arising from errors or omissions, if any, in this book, and are not responsible for accidents, incidents, personal injuries, damage to property or any other losses sustained by readers who engage in the activities described in this book.

This book is sold without warranties or guarantees of any kind, express or implied, and the authors and publisher disclaim any liability, loss or damage caused by the contents.

If you do not wish to be bound by these cautions and conditions, disagree with the foregoing disclaimer of liability, you may return this book for a full refund of the purchase price.

Dedicated to

Stephan Bianchi, Susan's fellow explorer;
Mary Franich Bignell;
and the memory of
Doug Kirby, for his love of life and all things Santa Cruz.

TABLE OF CONTENTS

THE WALTON LIGHTHOUSE STANDS 42 FEET TALL AT THE ENTRANCE
TO THE SANTA CRUZ SMALL CRAFT HARBOR.

ACKNOWLEDGMENTS

It is probably safe to say that at least 228 interesting, generous, creative and talented people helped us write and publish this book: docents, artists, librarians, museum staff, park rangers, journalists, historians, editors, graphic designers, proofreaders and our many friends and colleagues who offered ideas and support.

The intrepid Mardi Richmond, senior editor at Journeyworks Publishing, with the help of the talented Kate St. Clair and Janet Gellman, had the unenviable task of trying to bring cohesion and consistency to a manuscript that kept changing and growing. They did an amazing job. Eva Bernstein, who always takes on more than anyone can handle and still gets it done, provided the book design. Su Gatch deserves special thanks for stepping in at the last minute to design the cover and help get the manuscript ready for press. And, as always, thanks to the staff at Journeyworks for their support—especially Kate Clark for her creative ideas and feedback.

Although we've mentioned many sources of ideas and inspiration in our notes section, there are a few people who deserve additional thanks: Crystal Birns, an amazing resource for all things art related; Leslie Keedy, urban forester; Chris Lay, curator for the Natural History Collections at UCSC; Lisa Robinson, collections manager at the San Lorenzo Valley Museum; John Hibble, who opened our eyes to the history of Aptos and Rio del Mar; Eric Taylor of the Scotts Valley Historical Society; Ed Carnegie, director of the Swanton Pacific Railroad; retired fire chief Gene Friend; Loretta Estrada of the Rodgers House Committee; Jane Borg of the Pajaro Valley Historical Association; and Byrne Forest caretaker Jeff Helmer.

This county also has wonderful local historians and naturalists who have inspired us over the years: John Chase, Donald Clark, Geoffrey Dunn, Ross Gibson, Gary Griggs, Betty Lewis, Sandy Lydon, Frank Perry, Stan Stevens and Carolyn Swift.

Susan would like to thank Stephan Bianchi for his many helpful ideas, enthusiasm and companionship in exploring many of the "things" that appear in this book, and for his insightful comments about the manuscript. She also thanks Eva Bernstein for suggesting to Steven that the two of us write this book together.

Steven would never get anything done without his wife, Mary Franich Bignell. Since she's lived in Santa Cruz County all her life she was also an invaluable resource for ideas and feedback. Mary also created our subject index, a testament to her years of being a professional librarian. Steven also wants to thank his late friend Doug Kirby who was always a source of encouragement and inspiration.

We also want to acknowledge the efforts of the committed individuals who make it their mission to build, restore and champion things they believe are important to the experience of living here. We thank them for making Santa Cruz County a special place for all of us to enjoy and appreciate.

■ INTRODUCTION

Peering timidly up from a traffic island on the Westside of Santa Cruz are a bunch of tiny ceramic creatures. A red fox, a skunk and a tiny bunny nestle among banana slugs, lady bugs, birds, worms and lizards. How could it be that we had walked by this whimsical sculpture numerous times and never noticed it? We also learned that most of our friends had yet to see this delightful treasure. Stumbling upon this small but notable slice of Santa Cruz made us stop and think: "What else haven't we seen?" That question became the inspiration for this book and we set out on a multiyear quest to find, photograph and write about the many interesting, odd, beautiful and historic things that can be seen in Santa Cruz County.

Our goal in writing this book is to reintroduce the wonders of our diverse county to people who live here, as well as to introduce Santa Cruz County to new arrivals and visitors. A great benefit of writing this book was discovering, after living in town for a combined 65 years, how many things we didn't know about and had not yet seen. The more we looked, the more we found, and we realized that the hardest part of writing this book was deciding what not to include. Our list of interesting things to see that are not in the book is nearly as long as the list of things we included.

This book is not meant to be a history book. (For more history, check out our notes and selected bibliography for resources.) Nor is this book meant to be comprehensive. Despite being the second smallest of California's 58 counties (only San Francisco city/county is smaller), Santa Cruz County is one of the most varied, with a diverse geography and rich history. These 228 descriptions cannot begin to describe everything worthy of being seen in the county. But what we hope is that this book will be a stimulating resource and a reminder that no matter how long you have lived here, there are still new things to see. We encourage you to discover your own favorites—our hope is that you will be inspired to seek out new places throughout the county and boldly go where you haven't gone before.

Some of Steven's favorites: Blue Whale Skeleton, especially when Ms. Blue is lighted for the holidays (#69); Rock and Roll Jesus (#15); Heather Robyn Matthews' carved glass windows at Star of the Sea (#154); The Giant Hedge (#66); Pacific Migrations Interactive Map (#178); The Pink Maiden at the Aptos History Museum (#185); and the By the Strength of Our Hands exhibit (#203) at the California Agricultural Workers' History Center.

Some of Susan's favorites: The Farm at UCSC (#82); Paradise Park – Historic Site of California Powder Works (#94); The Old Alba Schoolhouse (#113); the many sights at the historic Wilder Ranch State Park complex (#127–130); Glaum Egg Ranch Egg Vending Machine (#190); Fruit Crate Label Murals in Watsonville (#195); and View from the Bluffs at La Selva Beach (#197).

While we have tried to include descriptions of objects and places that are likely to be permanent local sights, things do disappear. Shortly before we were ready for press, the domed Stone Castle at 1211 Fair Street in Santa Cruz, built by Raymond Kitchen, was torn down with little fanfare. The mission-era baptismal font in the Mission Chapel Garden was vandalized and moved indoors. And Michael McLaughlin's wonderful penguin sculptures, the Boys of Summer, that had been sitting on Pacific Avenue in Santa Cruz since 2009, migrated south to San Diego.

The descriptions are organized geographically into eight sections, from the rugged North Coast to Watsonville's fertile agricultural fields. The small towns in Mid-County are well represented, as are the historic lumber towns in the San Lorenzo Valley. UCSC gets its own section. And the vibrant city of Santa Cruz is broken out into Downtown, Westside and Eastside.

In the appendices you will find our notes, a selected bibliography, a list of names, addresses and contact information for all Santa Cruz County museums and art galleries, and a detailed subject index.

We encourage you to keep this book handy. If ever you find yourself feeling that there is nothing to do in Santa Cruz County, open the pages and start on a new adventure. You will be glad you did!

DOWNTOWN SANTA CRUZ & VICINITY

Downtown Santa Cruz is a mecca of shops, restaurants, amusements, museums and historical architecture.

This section includes Pacific Avenue and other Downtown streets, Beach Flats, the Boardwalk and the Santa Cruz Municipal Wharf, and the area around Harvey West Park.

1 SANTA CRUZ TOWN CLOCK

To many who live in Santa Cruz, the impressive Town Clock that stands at the hub of Downtown is the emotional center of the city, serving as a place for gatherings, celebrations and protests both planned and spontaneous. But the Town Clock also has a unique history. The clock dates to 1900 and originally sat atop the old Independent Order of Odd Fellows building on Pacific Avenue. When the building was remodeled in 1964, the clock was removed and remained in storage until the 1970s, when reinstalling it became the city's Bicentennial project. Restoration was a community-wide effort, partially supported by donations of money and labor from volunteers, businesses and labor unions. Together, they built a new brick base and mounted the clock at the top. The new tower and renovated clock were dedicated on July 4, 1976. The Town Clock survived

THE SANTA CRUZ TOWN CLOCK, JUST 10 MILES FROM THE EPICENTER, SURVIVED THE MAGNITUDE 6.9 LOMA PRIETA EARTHQUAKE.

the October 17, 1989, Loma Prieta earthquake that devastated Downtown Santa Cruz. It stopped running at exactly the moment the earthquake struck—the clock's hands frozen at 5:04 p.m. In a mood of optimism and survival, an emotional Town Clock relighting ceremony took place on December 2, 1989, amidst the rubble of collapsed buildings. A plaque at the base of the clock reads, "In memory of those who lost their lives in the Loma Prieta earthquake of Oct. 17, 1989. Shawn McCormick, Robin Lynn Ortiz, Catherine Trieman."

■ **The Town Clock is at the intersection of Pacific Avenue and Water Street, Santa Cruz.**

EARLY VIEWS OF SANTA CRUZ

Ever wondered what Santa Cruz looked like back in the 1800s? Within 100 yards of each other are three wonderful early images of Santa Cruz: one at Santa Cruz City Hall and two in the Santa Cruz Public Library's Downtown Branch.

2 SANTA CRUZ 1870

For a bird's-eye view of Santa Cruz in 1870, check out this 4-by-6-foot reproduction of a lithograph by artist C. B. Gifford. Downtown is a mere handful of streets running between large lots filled with orchards. Sailing ships and steamships are heading for piers, and horse-drawn wagons and carriages travel along the shore. And when looking at the original river basin of the meandering San Lorenzo River, you will

A CLOSE-UP VIEW OF A SMALL PORTION OF GIFFORD'S GREAT LITHOGRAPH

understand why Downtown Santa Cruz was destined for future floods. Twenty-six numbered references in the lower margin of the print identify prominent buildings and other landmarks, most of which have long since disappeared.

■ **The lithograph is located in the Information Technology office, Room 8, of the Santa Cruz City Hall at 809 Center Street, Santa Cruz.**

3 SANTA CRUZ 1892

Access to books, videos and the Internet is not the only great reason to go to the Downtown Santa Cruz Public Library. Above the stairway landing, near the second-floor entrance to the Young People's Room, is a 6-by-8-foot painting of Santa Cruz by renowned California painter Frank L. Heath. The view in this massive 1892 oil painting is from above the city near Graham Hill Road, looking across Downtown and out to the bay. You see the untamed San Lorenzo River, early bridges (including a former covered bridge where the Soquel Avenue Bridge now stands) and multiple

NOTICE THE COVERED BRIDGE IN THIS DETAIL FROM "CITY OF SANTA CRUZ."

piers stretching into the bay. Famous in its day, this painting was exhibited at the Chicago World's Fair in 1893 and at the St. Louis World's Fair in 1904. Entitled simply, "City of Santa Cruz," the painting, with its heavy and ornate gilt frame, is both an artistic and historic treasure.

■ **This painting is located in the Downtown Branch of the Santa Cruz Public Library at 224 Church Street, Santa Cruz.**

4 SANTA CRUZ 1906

As you enter the California History and Genealogy Room of the Downtown Branch of the Santa Cruz Public Library, take a look above the bookshelves on the left. In 1906, George Lawrence, a commercial photographer famous for his post-earthquake aerial photo San Francisco in Ruins, took the first aerial photographs of the Central Coast, including this four-frame panorama of Santa Cruz. Lawrence, assisted by five men, used a train of cargo kites to hoist a 50-pound camera along a steel cable 1,000 feet above Monterey Bay. Taken in the early summer from above West Cliff Drive, the almost 6-foot-wide, black-and-white photo shows Santa Cruz from the bay to the distant peak of Loma Prieta. Historian Peter Nurkse, in a wonderful article that can be found in the local history section of the library's website, painstakingly identifies more than 40 buildings and other sites visible in the photo. He points out that none of the three wharves in the photo still exists. The Jordan and Davis Wharf (aka Cowell Wharf) on the left, built in 1849, was destroyed by storms in 1907. The Railroad Wharf, the next wharf to the right, was torn down in 1922. (The existing Municipal Wharf was built in 1914, just east of the Railroad Wharf.) The smaller Pleasure Pier on the far right, used to bring seawater to the Boardwalk's old saltwater pool, was torn down in 1965. The city may have changed, but the curve of the bay is unmistakable. While you are in the California History Room, you may also want to browse the extensive Californiana and Genealogy collections or use the microfiche viewers to read local newspapers from as far back as 1854.

■ **This panorama is located in the Downtown Branch of the Santa Cruz Public Library at 224 Church Street, Santa Cruz.**

THOSE AREN'T SMUDGES, BUT WISPS OF SUMMER FOG LINGERING BELOW THE 1,000-FOOT LEVEL. THE PHOTO IS BELIEVED TO HAVE BEEN TAKEN ON JUNE 24, 1906. (PHOTO COURTESY OF THE LIBRARY OF CONGRESS)

5 POST OFFICE MURALS

Inside the Downtown Santa Cruz Post Office is a series of colorful, Depression-era murals depicting the main industries of Santa Cruz at the time. In 1935, the federal government's Works Progress Administration (WPA) was actively creating public project jobs in an effort to stimulate the economy. Local artist Henrietta Shore was hired in 1936 to paint the four post office murals: "Limestone Quarries," "Fishing

"CABBAGE CULTURE" BY HENRIETTA SHORE

Industry," "Artichoke Raising" and "Cabbage Culture." These bright, oil-on-canvas paintings emphasize the dignity of labor and are in a period style similar to that of other well-known muralists of the day such as Diego Rivera and José Clemente Orozco, both friends of Shore.

6 COMPASS ROSE

Did you know that Santa Cruz has sister cities? To see where they are located, visit the large compass rose made of pink and gray granite set in the pavement next to the Downtown Santa Cruz Post Office. A compass rose is a figure designed to show the orientations of north, east, south, west and their intermediate points. This compass rose points to the locations of five of Santa Cruz's sister cities: Puerto la Cruz, Venezuela; Shingu, Japan; Sestri Levanti, Italy; Alushta, Crimea, Ukraine; and Jinotepe, Nicaragua. Santa Cruz de Tenerife, Spain is not shown.

■ **The Santa Cruz Post Office is located at 850 Front Street.**

FIVE SANTA CRUZ SISTER CITIES ARE MARKED ON THE COMPASS ROSE.

7 WORLD WAR I MEMORIAL

Forty-two men and two women from Santa Cruz died while in military service during World War I. The nesting brass eagle, on top of the tall granite pedestal at the north end of Pacific Avenue, commemorates their sacrifice. The memorial was installed on Memorial Day in 1928, as the Santa Cruz Municipal Band played "Stars and Stripes Forever." A bronze plaque on one side of the memorial pedestal lists the names of the fallen.

■ **The memorial is in the plaza at the convergence of Pacific Avenue and Front Street.**

DEDICATED TO THE SOLDIERS AND SAILORS OF ALL WARS

8 COLLATERAL DAMAGE: A REALITY OF WAR

COLLATERAL DAMAGE: A REALITY OF WAR

Peace activism has long had an active presence in Santa Cruz and the sculpture next to the Town Clock expresses that conviction. Collateral Damage: A Reality of War depicts the human agony of innocents as the result of war. Artist E. A. Chase donated his sculpture to commemorate the 50th anniversary of the atomic bombing of Hiroshima and Nagasaki. The artist described the statue as depicting "a man, woman and child frozen in that final embrace before utter destruction." The sculpture's installation was controversial at the time because of its antiwar message and concerns that it dishonored war veterans. A plaque at the base of the work reads, "In Memory of Civilians Who Have Died in All Wars." It is accompanied by a list of supporters and contributors who, the plaque says, actively "Wage Peace."

■ **The sculpture is located at the intersection of Pacific Avenue and Water Street, next to the Town Clock.**

9 MOVIE STAR FOOTPRINTS

You don't have to travel to Hollywood to see movie stars' footprints, handprints and autographs immortalized in concrete. Instead, visit the patio in front of the Nickelodeon movie theatre to see the Santa Cruz version of Grauman's Chinese Theatre's famous forecourt. Pressed in the pavement in front of the "The Nick" are the handprints and footprints of two Santa Cruz native sons, movie stars Rory Calhoun and Walter Reed, who were best known in the 1940s and '50s. The darkly handsome Rory Calhoun, who spent part of his childhood in Santa Cruz, was a famous leading man in many movies and television programs, including acting alongside Marilyn Monroe in *How to Marry a Millionaire* and *River of No Return*. Character actor Walter Reed performed in hundreds of films and television programs, then retired from acting to settle in Santa Cruz in the late 1960s. Bronze plaques embedded in the cement commemorate September 19, 1991, as Rory Calhoun Day and July 14, 2001, as Walter Reed Day; both declared such by Resolution of the City and County of Santa Cruz.

■ **The Nickelodeon is located at 210 Lincoln Street, Santa Cruz.**

RORY CALHOUN'S HANDPRINTS AND FOOTPRINTS

DEL MAR MOVIE PALACE

Going to the movies in the 1930s was a luxurious experience heightened by the elaborate architecture of theatres of that time. Referred to as movie palaces, theatres were designed to make the visitor feel like royalty. The fantastic Art Deco Del Mar Theatre first opened its doors in 1936 with the premiere showing of Warner Brothers' *China Clipper*. The *Santa Cruz Sentinel* newspaper reported, "Six usherettes, all blondes, in attractive red uniforms, and three ushers in white sports coats showed the guests to their seats." Sadly, after years of decline, the curtains closed in 1999 and the theatre was soon referred to as a "rotten tooth" in the mouth of Downtown. But that was not the end of the story. In a partnership between the City of Santa Cruz, developers, and the owners of the established local art house theatre, the Nickelodeon, the doors of the Del Mar reopened in 2002. Today the Del Mar is again the palace of days gone by. The red-and-green neon marquee, festooned with stars and seashells, flashes brightly on Pacific Avenue. Inside, the renovated grand auditorium awes with gilded female figures that rise halfway up the wall on both sides of the movie screen and plush velvet curtains that open to reveal today's movie magic.

■ **The Del Mar is located at 1124 Pacific Avenue, Santa Cruz.**

THE DEL MAR MARQUEE ON PACIFIC AVENUE

11 THE OCTAGON

Octagonal buildings were popular in the late 19th century but few of these rare structures survive today. Santa Cruz is lucky to have a wonderful example of this form of architecture. Built in 1882, the Octagon is a small, but grand, red brick building that was used as the Santa Cruz County Hall of Records until 1968. Fortunately, the county recognized it as being too important an architectural element of Downtown Santa Cruz to tear down, and a preservation effort led to its conversion to a new use. Today the Octagon is a coffeehouse and satellite gallery for the neighboring Museum of Art and History (MAH), which regularly changes the art on display to feature local artists.

■ **The Octagon is at 118 Cooper Street at Front Street, Santa Cruz.**

THE OCTAGON MUSEUM GALLERY AND COFFEEHOUSE

12 ART AT THE COUNTY BUILDING

Did you know the County Government Center hosts a free art gallery? Four annual art displays, on the first and fifth floors of the building, bring local art directly to the community. Sponsored by the Arts Council and the County Department of Parks, Open Space and Cultural Services, each 10-week show presents work from five Santa Cruz County artists. Wall displays include paintings, prints, drawings and photographs, while ceramics, jewelry and other fine crafts are exhibited in three 8-foot-long display cases. Every April and May, there is also an exhibit of children's work produced through the Arts Council's arts education program. A large exhibit area on the first floor, called the Community Wall, showcases displays from local community groups. If you ever need to visit the center to pick up a ballot, marriage license or property tax bill, take some extra time to wander the halls and enjoy the art on display.

■ **The County Government Center is located at 701 Ocean Street, Santa Cruz.**

THE FIFTH-FLOOR GALLERY AT THE COUNTY BUILDING

13 THE MUSEUM OF ART AND HISTORY

A sculpture of a giant letter *M* next to a big red ball at the corner of Cathcart and Front Streets leads you to the innovative Museum of Art and History (MAH) at the McPherson Center. If you want to experience local contemporary art and get a fascinating look at the history of Santa Cruz County, this is the place to visit. Although the largest museum in the county, it is divided into a series of small galleries and is never overwhelming. The second-floor gallery houses the long-term exhibit "Where the Redwoods Meet the Sea: A History of Santa Cruz County and Its People." This gallery presents photos and artifacts from the days of the early native peoples through the 20th century. You will see wonderful displays

WELCOME TO THE MUSEUM.

on the Mission period, the logging industry, the early Boardwalk and other tourist amusements. This gallery also features a history of the Scotts Valley Tree Circus, including an 8-foot-tall preserved trunk of one of the famous arbor-sculpted trees.

READ THIS BOY'S 1911 DIARY ENTRIES ABOUT GROWING UP IN SANTA CRUZ.

(See page 104 for the story of the Tree Circus in Scotts Valley.) The museum's three galleries (one on every floor) house rotating exhibits of creative and inspiring works including paintings, ceramics and sculpture, often by local artists and artisans. The small Blanchard Sculpture Garden on the third floor not only showcases outdoor sculpture, but also provides wonderful views of the city and the Santa Cruz Mountains. Additional art can be seen on the landings, in the lobbies and in a small shop with one-of-a-kind gifts off the atrium entrance. The constantly changing exhibits make this museum always worth a visit.

■ **The Museum of Art and History is located at 705 Front Street, in Downtown Santa Cruz.**

14 TOM SCRIBNER STATUE

Have you ever wondered about the bronze statue on Pacific Avenue of an elderly man, wearing a bowler hat and suspenders, playing a saw? It is the likeness of Tom Scribner, a longtime Downtown fixture who played his musical saw for anyone who would listen. Tom performed almost every day during the 1970s and early 1980s, until his death in 1982. Most who had the chance to hear him say that his playing was less compelling than his entertaining character, although he is known to have played with famous musicians such as Neil Young, George Harrison and Leon Russell. Originally a lumberjack in Minnesota, Scribner was a labor organizer with

the Industrial Workers of the World (the "Wobblies") and a member of the Communist Party. The Wobblies were active from 1905 until World War I and aspired to organize unskilled workers around the world into "One Big Union." In Santa Cruz, Scribner was a counter-culture celebrity, editor, and founder of the annual Musical Saw Festival, which continues to take place at Felton's Roaring Camp. Artist Marghe McMahon created the sculpture in the late '70s, donating her own money toward the costs. The statue is in front of what was once the St. George Hotel, Scribner's old residence and where he spent most of his time entertaining passers-by.

■ **You will find the statue in front of Bookshop Santa Cruz, at 1500 Pacific Avenue, Santa Cruz.**

TOM SCRIBNER, A COUNTER-CULTURE CELEBRITY

15 ROCK AND ROLL JESUS

Inside, above the main entrance to the legendary Catalyst nightclub, is a statue of Jesus unlike any you have ever seen. Three feet tall and enclosed in plexiglass, this

JESUS PLAYING HIS FENDER STRATOCASTER

bearded, blue-eyed Jesus is wearing a blue tunic and purple robe, and on his head is a crown of thorns. His left hand holds an electric guitar. His right hand is raised, holding a guitar pick, ready to strum. And surrounding him are neon lights that bathe him in a psychedelic pink glow. The statue came from a church in Nicaragua, as a gift to Catalyst owner Randall Kane, sometime in the '80s. Kane then hired a local artist to create and add the guitar to the statue. This Jesus is serene and strong and, despite the unusual accessories, commands respect. Walk into the Catalyst and make sure you look up to check out who is watching over you.

■ **The Catalyst is located at 1011 Pacific Avenue, Santa Cruz.**

16 PACIFIC AVENUE SCULPTURES

One of the many treats of wandering along Pacific Avenue in Downtown Santa Cruz is viewing the sculptures spaced every few hundred feet. Untitled Clevis #2 by Harold Moodie is the graceful abstract steel sculpture in front of the Cooper House that children and adults have sat and climbed on for more than 20 years. It is part of the collection of sculptures selected by public vote and installed along Pacific Avenue after the 1989 Loma Prieta earthquake. Other permanent works include Kimono Sigh by Coeleen Kiebert and the bright orange Cube by Gary Dwyer. Pacific Avenue also

hosts SculpTOUR, a rotating gallery of sculpture on loan to the city. Installations include Moto Ohtake's delicate kinetic sculpture Aero #7 and the tall, swirling Oceanic Life Spiral by Kirk McNeill. With well over a dozen sculptures on Pacific Avenue, see how many you can find.

■ **The sculptures are located along Pacific Avenue in Downtown Santa Cruz.**

THIS IS SCULPTURE YOU CAN SIT AND CLIMB ON.

17 CITY HALL GARDENS

The gardens at Santa Cruz City Hall are spectacular at any time of year and are full of many unusual subtropical plants and trees that thrive in the mild Santa Cruz climate. If you are interested in plants, you will want to spend some time exploring here. One of the most interesting trees in the gardens is an unusually shaped Canary Island date palm. A bird probably planted this tree, which explains its location directly underneath the building's eave. The palm, estimated to be 50 or 60 years old, arches elegantly out from under the shelter of the eave, reaching toward the sun. There is also a citrus courtyard with a bubbling fountain at its center. This is an especially pleasant spot to sit when the trees are in bloom, perfuming the air with their scent. Nearby is a small but thriving cactus garden with many large plants. Don't miss the rose garden planted on the Locust Street side of the building. There are many varieties here to admire when the roses are in bloom.

■ **Santa Cruz City Hall is located at 809 Center Street, Santa Cruz.**

CANARY ISLAND DATE PALM AT SANTA CRUZ CITY HALL

18 1930 WHARF ENTRANCE PLAN

If you are interested in seeing an artistic rendering of one of the many plans developed for the Santa Cruz waterfront that was never built, pay a visit to the Santa Cruz City Planning Department office at city hall. Here you will see a large-scale watercolor of an elaborate entrance to the Santa Cruz Municipal Wharf that was proposed in 1930. The artwork measures 2 by 6 feet and shows an impressive two-story, horseshoe-shaped promenade anchored by a

1930 PROPOSED ENTRANCE TO THE SANTA CRUZ WHARF

grand 132-foot tower entrance to the Wharf. Local architect Lee Dill Esty designed the entrance in the Mission style, a popular architectural style at the time. Esty was well known locally, having designed the Chaminade Boys School, now the Chaminade Resort & Spa, and the Pogonip Clubhouse. The image is a fascinating view of what might have been.

■ **The Santa Cruz City Planning Department office is located at 809 Center Street, Santa Cruz.**

19 GRANIZO MURAL AT THE CIVIC

In the rush to get to your seats in the Santa Cruz Civic Auditorium, you may not notice the tile mural over the four main entrance doors. Designed by Guillermo Wagner Granizo, one of the world's leading ceramic muralists, it was donated to the city by the artist in 1981. This 6-by-12-foot mural, comprised of 108 tiles, uses bright colors and geometric shapes to create a festive depiction of typical Civic Auditorium events: beauty pageants, book sales, roller derby contests, basketball games, ballets,

body-building contests, antinuclear demonstrations, rock concerts and more. It contains both religious symbolism from Granizo's Central American childhood and whimsical touches such as balloons, cats and clowns. See if you can find the naked streaker running across the stage.

■ **You can find the mural above the interior entrance to the Santa Cruz Civic Auditorium, located at 307 Church Street, Santa Cruz.**

GRANIZO'S MURALS ARE FOUND WORLDWIDE.

THE MURALS OF SANTA CRUZ

Santa Cruz is home to more than 30 mural artists, and murals have become an integral part of the artistic culture of the city. In 1994, the Redevelopment Agency began sponsoring mural projects by providing grant incentives to local business and property owners. There are now more than 21 murals in the City of Santa Cruz with more being added on a regular basis. They can be found along alleys, on side streets, and on the walls of large corner buildings. John Pugh's "Bay in a Bottle," on the wall of the Shopper's Corner grocery store at Soquel and Branciforte Avenues, celebrates Spanish explorer Sebastian Vizcaino's first view of Monterey Bay. Ann Thiermann's "A Peaceful Pawse" decorates Pearl Alley. Artist James Aschbacher's whimsical images can be found along Plaza Lane, and at the corner of Walnut Avenue and Cedar Street. A map of Downtown murals and other public art is available from the Santa Cruz City Arts Commission at 337 Locust Street. A few of our favorites are shown below.

■ **The murals are located throughout Santa Cruz.**

ANDY'S AUTO

This trompe l'oeil (trick the eye) on the side wall of Andy's Auto Supply was created by artists Herb Leippe and Kenna Allen in 1999 and is a local favorite. Its street scene features pedestrians and realistic parked cars, including a Chevy Corvette.

ON MAPLE STREET NEAR PACIFIC AVENUE

OLD SCHOOL SHOES

Artist Brian Barneclo, who specializes in large-scale murals (his famous "Food Chain" mural in San Francisco is 25 by 225 feet) painted this colorful ode to Santa Cruz on the side of Old School Shoes in 2009.

ON CATHCART STREET NEAR PACIFIC AVENUE

JAZZ ALLEY

Five jazz greats, all who have performed regularly in Santa Cruz, have been immortalized in a 70-foot mural by Santa Cruz artist Marvin Plummer. Giant portraits of singer Betty Carter, trumpeter Roy Hargrove, violinist Regina Carter, guitarist John Scofield and bassist Christian McBride point the way from Pacific

ON BIRCH LANE BETWEEN CEDAR STREET AND PACIFIC AVENUE

Avenue to the renowned Kuumbwa Jazz Center farther down the alley. Since 1975, the Kuumbwa Jazz Center has been showcasing some of the world's greatest jazz artists and these five performers were chosen because of their close ties to the Santa Cruz jazz scene.

MURAL OF SANTA CRUZ IN 1911

Take a look at Ann Thiermann's imaginative trompe l'oeil mural on Locust Street and see how she evokes Santa Cruz life at the beginning of the 20th century. The American flag on the old Santa Cruz County Bank building has 46 stars. A horseless carriage and a horse-drawn carriage both share Pacific Avenue with a streetcar. Women wear long dresses and everyone wears hats. Fred Swanton, who built the original boardwalk, is shown sitting on a bench reading the *Sentinel,* and the great architect William H. Weeks can be seen in the window of the People's Bank, which he designed in 1911. Writer and conservationist Josephine McCracken is entering the old *Sentinel* newspaper offices. Although musical saw player Tom Scribner was only 12 years old in 1911, Thiermann used artistic license to include his iconic image.

ON LOCUST STREET BEHIND 1515 PACIFIC AVENUE

21 WALNUT AVENUE VICTORIANS

One of the best places to see Santa Cruz homes that date from the late 19th and early 20th centuries is a two-block stretch of Walnut Avenue near Downtown Santa Cruz. Wealthy and prominent citizens built their homes on this tree-lined street. Every house is unique and many bear the city's distinctive oval blue plaque that lists the names of the original owner and architect. You can see various styles and combinations of styles including Italianate (1860–1910), Eastlake and Stick-Eastlake (1880s), Queen Anne (1885–1900) and Colonial Revival (1895–1910). Don't miss the elegant Queen Anne home built for District Attorney Carl E. Lindsay in 1895 at 219 Walnut Avenue. It has a striking corner tower and arched entrance. Frederick Hihn built the impressive Italianate home with Gothic Revival details at 249 Walnut Avenue for his daughter in 1870 after she married hardware merchant William T. Cope. Even the smaller homes on this street have a dignified presence, such as the Italianate cottage at 241 Walnut Avenue. If you have the time, wander a little farther. There are many historic homes on nearby streets.

■ **These homes are located on Walnut Avenue between Center and Rincon Streets.**

QUEEN ANNE AT 219 WALNUT AVENUE

COPE HOUSE AT 249 WALNUT AVENUE

22 LINCOLN COURT

A new type of housing was introduced in California in the early part of the 20th century: the bungalow court. Built between 1905 and 1920, Lincoln Court is composed of

ENTRANCE FROM LINCOLN STREET

a cluster of tiny bungalows built in a fusion of Craftsman and Colonial styles around a common courtyard, and is one of the few remaining examples of this type of architecture in Santa Cruz. Local architect and landscape designer Michael J. O'Hearn, who believed the garden was "an outside room," restored the cottages after the 1989 Loma Prieta earthquake and created shared gardens to encourage social interaction and a sense of community. Lincoln Court's picturesque and compact cottages are quaint in themselves, but the lush plantings create a lovely landscape that provides both beauty and privacy for the residents. A narrow and curving path disappears into the greenery from the entrance to the court on Lincoln Street and connects with New Street at the back. The courtyard is private, but you can still appreciate the homes and garden as you peer down the path.

■ **Lincoln Court is located at 315–323 Lincoln Street, Santa Cruz.**

23 BUNYA-BUNYA TREE

Ever heard of a bunya-bunya tree? This type of tree was around before dinosaurs roamed the earth, and you can take a look at a very large and old bunya-bunya at 304 Walnut Avenue. This towering bunya-bunya is believed to be more than 100 years old and has been a city Heritage Tree since 1977. The bark of this tree has a strangely rumpled appearance and the branches are sharp and spiky. You definitely do not want one to fall on your head! This evergreen coniferous tree is native to southeast Queensland, Australia, and was sacred to the Aboriginal people. It was also a favorite in gardens in California during Victorian times. Now that you know what to look for, you will notice large bunya-bunyas in front of many historic homes in Santa Cruz.

■ **This bunya-bunya tree is located at 304 Walnut Avenue, Santa Cruz.**

BUNYA-BUNYA TREE

HISTORIC STAIRCASES

Santa Cruz sits on a series of bluffs that made pedestrian access challenging as the city grew. Sometimes the shortest way is straight up, so early in the city's history a network of staircases was built to make foot travel easier. Many of these staircases still exist and are in use today. Walking up the steps will reward you with broad views of the City of Santa Cruz and the Monterey Bay. Here are a few staircases you might consider exploring.

■ **All are located in Downtown Santa Cruz.**

SCHOOL STREET STEPS

This staircase will take you from North Pacific Avenue to School Street above, site of Mission Santa Cruz, Holy Cross Church and Mission Plaza. Halfway up you will be treated to a bird's-eye view of the Town Clock and Downtown Santa Cruz.

PINE PLACE STEPS

You will find the Pine Place steps on Chestnut Street across from the city hall parking lot. The steps lead from Chestnut Street to Pine Place and Locust Street

DOWNTOWN SANTA CRUZ FROM
SCHOOL STREET STEPS

above. From here, you are only a short walk to Mission Street. At the top of the walkway, in one of Santa Cruz's oldest neighborhoods, you will find several lovely Victorian and Craftsman-style homes as well as the very interesting International-style Pine Place Apartments, built in 1937.

PINE PLACE APARTMENTS

WALNUT AVENUE STEPS

Two sets of staircases lead from Walnut Avenue (between Rincon Street and Santa Cruz High School) to the neighborhood above. Take the steps to the right and you will find yourself at Towne Terrace with a view toward Downtown. The staircase to the left will lead you past an apartment building to Grover Lane.

WALNUT AVENUE STEPS

HISTORIC GREEN STREET HOMES

A steep walk up Green Street from the edge of Downtown will present you with a quick overview of the rich and varied history of Santa Cruz architecture. In less than 200 yards, you'll see five distinctly different, beautiful and well-preserved examples

of mid-1800s to early 1900s building styles. At the top of the hill on the left at 123 Green Street, you'll see the Italianate Reynolds House. It was originally built in 1850 as a Methodist Church—the first Protestant church building in Santa Cruz. It was later moved to its present location on Green Street and remodeled. Farther on the left is the Otis

THE OTIS LONGLEY HOUSE HAS A WONDERFUL PORCH WITH BALUSTRADE.

Longley House, a white Gothic Revival built around 1868, followed by a stunning dark red 1905 Colonial Revival. On the right side of the street, at 120 Green Street, you'll see a magnificent Spanish Colonial Revival built in 1922–1924 by William H. Weeks (who also designed Santa Cruz High School, the Cocoanut Grove, and the Santa Cruz and Watsonville Carnegie Libraries). Farther on the right, at 134 Green

Street, is a beautifully landscaped Craftsman Bungalow that was built around 1915 with exposed rafters, a stone chimney and garden walls. The steep climb will be worth it, though you may be left with house-envy after seeing these beautiful and historic homes.

■ **You will find Green Street near the intersection of Union and Chestnut Streets, Santa Cruz.**

ARCHITECT WILLIAM H. WEEKS DESIGNED THIS
SPANISH COLONIAL REVIVAL FOR THE LEASK FAMILY.

MISIÓN LA EXALTACIÓN DE LA SANTA CRUZ

Misión la Exaltación de la Santa Cruz was consecrated in August 1791, the 12th Franciscan mission in the Alta California mission chain. At its peak in 1830, Mission Santa Cruz was a community of more than 30 buildings including workshops, storage buildings and living quarters for priests, soldiers and native people who had joined the mission. Mission Santa Cruz was secularized in 1834, and in 1857 after a long period of neglect, a severe earthquake finally destroyed the buildings. Soon afterward, property ownership was returned to the Catholic Church. In 1889, the current Holy Cross Church was built on the foundation of the previous adobe church. While only remnants of the original mission still exist, this historic area offers several points of interest for you to visit.

■ **The historic area of Misión la Exaltación de la Santa Cruz is located around Mission Plaza, at 126 High Street, Santa Cruz.**

---

26 MISSION PLAZA

Mission Plaza, the large quadrangle in front of Holy Cross Church, was the center of the former mission complex. Today, Mission Plaza is a beautiful open space with a large fountain at its center surrounded by benches, mature trees and lush lawn. It is the best starting point for your tour of the area.

27 MISSION BELL

At noon and at 6 p.m. every day, much of Santa Cruz can hear the tolling of the Holy Cross Church bell. Not many know that the church's single bell was recast in San Francisco in 1888 from three surviving old bells of the original mission church. Money to remake the 1,500-pound bell was donated by Mrs. Bernard Peyton, who made the gift to the church as a memorial to her deceased son, Henry Peyton.

MISSION PLAZA AND HOLY CROSS CHURCH

28 NEARY-RODRIGUEZ ADOBE

This modest adobe is the only surviving structure of the original Misión la Exaltación de la Santa Cruz. Native people who had joined the mission built this 130-foot-long adobe between 1822 and 1824 to house their families. After Mission Santa Cruz was secularized, Californios (California-born Mexican families) lived in the building until 1959, when it was purchased by the State of California. The exterior of the adobe has been restored to the way it looked in 1840. Inside, you can tour the seven remaining rooms, several of which have been set to tell the story of the different peoples who lived here over a span of 159 years. In one room, you can see how native

A DISPLAY OF NATIVE AMERICAN LIFE IN THE ADOBE

people lived. Another room represents the early occupancy of the Californio families. In another you can see a model of the mission compound at its height in 1830. This is a unique structure showing many fascinating layers of early Santa Cruz history.

■ **Santa Cruz Mission State Park is at 144 School Street, one block off Mission Plaza, in Santa Cruz.**

THIS ADOBE IS THE LAST REMAINING ORIGINAL BUILDING OF MISSION SANTA CRUZ.

SANTA CRUZ MISSION CHAPEL AND RELIQUARY

The charming Santa Cruz Mission Chapel and Reliquary, built in 1932, is an approximate one-half-scale replica of the Mission Santa Cruz adobe church of the late 1700s. This building contains the oldest and most valuable treasures from early mission history, including a painting that is the only known image of the mission church from this period. Architects based their plans for the replica on the painting by Frenchman

A REPLICA OF THE ORIGINAL MISSION CHURCH

Léon Trousset and on surviving mission records. A number of religious paintings and statues dating from the mid-19th century hang in the small chapel where daily masses are held. In the reliquary, you will find mission-era vestments made from still colorful Chinese silk that were worn by priests for ceremonies from 1792 to 1834.

There are also sacred vessels used in the Catholic Mass, paintings, silver candlesticks, leather-bound books and a chalice used by Father Junipero Serra, founder of the Alta California missions. Gladys Sullivan Doyle donated funds for construction of the replica, and she and her son, Peter Doyle, are buried under the bell tower.

■ **The Santa Cruz Mission Chapel and Reliquary is located at 130 Emmet Street, Santa Cruz.**

THE MISSION CHAPEL REPLICA WAS BUILT IN 1932.

MISSION CHAPEL GARDEN

Behind the Santa Cruz Mission Chapel and Reliquary is a tiny but lovely garden. This peaceful sanctuary is accessible from either the chapel or the reliquary and is a quiet place to stop, pray or meditate. In the center of the garden is an octagonal fountain with floating lilies. Beyond, against the garden wall, is a statue of Father Junipero Serra. There is other statuary in the garden, including a bronze Mary Magdalene standing on a tall pedestal.

■ **The garden is at 130 Emmet Street, Santa Cruz.**

FATHER JUNIPERO SERRA, FOUNDER OF THE CALIFORNIA MISSIONS

THE SANTA CRUZ MISSION CHAPEL GARDEN

31 HOLY CROSS CHURCH CEILING

One of the most visible landmarks in Santa Cruz is the picturesque Holy Cross Church. When you enter the church, your gaze will immediately rise up to the magnificent paintings that cover the ceiling. These works are by Italian-born San Francisco artist Attilio Moretti (1851–1915). The paintings above the nave are of the apostles; above the choir loft are two patrons of music, Saint Cecilia, who holds a miniature organ, and King David, who holds a harp. Each figure is set within a painted Gothic arch and is surrounded by decorative images of flowers and plants. The paintings were done on canvas and then glued in place against the ceiling around 1908. They were cleaned and restored in 1984. The church is open to the public only during Mass and other scheduled events.

■ **Holy Cross Church is located at 126 High Street, Santa Cruz.**

THE CEILING OF HOLY CROSS CHURCH

32 HOLY CROSS ARCH

Directly in front of the entrance to Holy Cross Church you will find an imposing Gothic-style arch. Constructed in 1891, the arch commemorated the 100-year anniversary of Mission Santa Cruz. Composed of granite blocks and a series of pointed arches, the 120-year-old gateway is an impressive presence.

ONE-HUNDRED-YEAR ANNIVERSARY COMMEMORATIVE ARCH

33 OLDEST FRAME HOUSE IN SANTA CRUZ

Built around 1850 by Francisco Alzina, the first sheriff in Santa Cruz County after statehood, this dark red clapboard house near Holy Cross Church is considered to be the oldest wood-frame house in Santa Cruz. It is a classic saltbox, with an asymmetrical pitched roof that is steep in the front with a long slope down to the back, creating two stories in the front and one story in the rear. It faces Mission Plaza, which is the oldest public park in the county.

■ **This private home is located at 107 Sylvar Street across from Mission Plaza Park, Santa Cruz.**

COLONIAL-STYLE SALTBOX HOUSES ORIGINATED IN NEW ENGLAND.

34 TANNERY ARTS CENTER

If you like to see artists at work, you'll want to pay a visit to the 8.2-acre Tannery Arts Center (TAC) located in the historic former Salz Tannery buildings on the San Lorenzo River. Salz Tannery closed in 2001 after 145 years of operation. In a joint project with the City of Santa Cruz, TAC opened 100 units of newly constructed live-work housing for artists and their families in 2009. Next, the Digital Media and Creative Arts Center opened in 2012. It is comprised of 25,000 square feet of working studio space. This space was created by renovating the red barnlike historic buildings of the old tannery factory. Tenants include an art gallery and artists of many disciplines such as jewelry, ceramics, printmaking, glass making, painting, book arts, animation, leatherwork, sculpture, photography and dance. Many of these studios are open to visitors when artists are at work and some offer classes to the public. There is also a wonderful café located on an inner courtyard. Nearby you will find a series of exhibits explaining the history of the tannery, including photos by famed photographer Ansel Adams taken during his visit here in 1955. The final phase of TAC is the construction of the Performing Arts Center, which will include a 200-seat theater for local dance, drama, film and music performances. This will be the home of the Santa Cruz Ballet Theatre, a pre-professional company of dancers, ranging in age from 8 to 20. Great times to visit TAC are during monthly First Friday and First Saturday events, as well as during special festivals and Santa Cruz's annual Open Studios.

■ **The Tannery Arts Center is located at 1050 River Street near the intersection of Highways 1 and 9, in Santa Cruz.**

CAFÉ AND COURTYARD NEXT TO ARTIST STUDIOS

35 TOTEM POLE AND WOODEN INDIANS

THE TOTEM POLE

In 1955, local lumberman Harvey West gave Santa Cruz the land for what eventually became the 50-acre Harvey West Park. In addition to ball fields, playgrounds and picnic areas, West's legacy also includes nine carved wooden Indians, a 40-foot-tall totem pole, as well as a steam train engine from from the early 20th century. The totem pole stands in front of the Great Western Overland Stage building in the heart of the park. Commissioned by West in the early 1960s, it was carved by an itinerant wood sculptor named Jim Gallagher. Although Gallagher did not carve authentic Native American totemic figures, his friendly totem creatures invite young and old to enjoy the expansive park. Peer inside the large windows of the adjacent Overland Stage building to see a bright red stagecoach, an old wooden sign that reads, "The Harvey West Indian Collection, Largest in the Nation, 1960," and seven carved and colorfully painted life-sized wooden Indians. These figures were created at a time when American Indians were often depicted in a stereotypical and insensitive fashion and the carvings reflect pre-civil-rights-era sensibilities. There is a seated chief, three young warriors and three women carrying infants on their backs. Nearby, in front of the Harvey West Park administration building, stand two more wooden warriors. It is believed that at least some of these wooden Indians were also carved by Jim Gallagher, who was known across the country for his wooden "crossed-eyed Indians."

■ **The carvings and totem pole are located in the heart of Harvey West Park, 326 Evergreen Street, Santa Cruz.**

36 ENGINE #1298

THIS TRAIN ENGINE SITS MAJESTICALLY IN THE FIELD.

Although kids can no longer climb onto this old train engine, it still sits proudly on display behind a short wooden fence at Harvey West Park. This Southern Pacific steam engine was one of 27 of its type built by Baldwin Locomotive Works in Philadelphia in 1913 and 1917. For 60 years, from 1880 to 1940, Southern Pacific trains provided freight and passenger service between Santa Cruz and Los Gatos. If you are nearby, stop to pay your respects to this symbol of a bygone era.

■ **The train engine is located in the Harvey West Park picnic area behind the pool.**

37 EVERGREEN CEMETERY

A visit to Evergreen Cemetery is a brief lesson in local history. The cemetery was established in 1850 as one of the first Protestant cemeteries in California and original plans were for 241 gravesites. Today, Evergreen Cemetery is the final resting place for more than 2,000 people including pioneers, Civil War veterans, Chinese laborers and early prominent Santa Cruz citizens. The cemetery is maintained by the Museum of Art and History, and you can join one of their docent-led tours or you can take your own tour. Start your visit at the main entrance. To the far left is the Masonic plot, where members of the California coast's fourth lodge are buried. To the right of that is the Grand Army of the Republic plot, for local Civil War veterans. At the top of the hill is the Chinese burial ground and below that is potter's field, site of unmarked graves of people too poor to afford burial. The rest of the cemetery contains private burial plots that include some recognizable and historic Santa Cruz names. Louden Nelson, a former slave who donated his land to the school district and the namesake of Louden Nelson Community Center, is buried here. Isaac Graham, for whom Graham Hill Road was named, is also buried here. The grave of baby Julia Arcan is the earliest recorded burial in the cemetery. Her family's wagon train was stranded in Death Valley in 1849 and gave the famous valley its name.

■ **The cemetery is located on Evergreen Street, next to Harvey West Park, Santa Cruz.**

MAIN ENTRANCE TO EVERGREEN CEMETERY

38 POGONIP CLUBHOUSE

Pogonip, part of the City of Santa Cruz greenbelt, has 640 acres of meadows, woodlands, creeks and approximately 8 miles of hiking trails. If you go for a walk in the lower part of the park, you may wonder about the dilapidated building on a grassy hillside with a panoramic view of Santa Cruz and the Monterey Bay. This is the Pogonip Clubhouse, built by local entrepreneur Fred Swanton and opened in 1912, along with an 18-hole golf course. Swanton went into bankruptcy the following year, but the course continued as the Santa Cruz Golf and Country Club until the mid-1930s. In 1936, it was reopened as the Pogonip Polo Club, home of first United States Women's Polo Association. Later a private social club, it was also used as a set in three different movies, including the 1986 movie *The Lost Boys*. Ultimately, the cost of restoring the building became too great and the stables were demolished, the swimming pool filled in and finally, the building was condemned. In 1989, the property was purchased by the City of Santa Cruz. Many hoped the clubhouse would be restored as a gathering place for visitors but so far, funding has not been available. You can take one of several trails to reach the clubhouse, which remains, despite its deteriorated condition, a great example of rustic resort architecture.

■ **The clubhouse is a short walk from the Golf Club Drive entrance to Pogonip, Santa Cruz.**

POGONIP CLUBHOUSE AWAITS RESTORATION.

SANTA CRUZ MEMORIAL PARK HISTORY WALK

In 1862, the Independent Order of Odd Fellows founded the cemetery that is known today as Santa Cruz Memorial Park. Many noted Santa Cruz figures are buried here, including early pioneers and colorful personalities. Some of their family names are familiar to us as names of local streets and geographic sites. The park has put together a booklet and map, aptly entitled "A Walk Through Time," which guides visitors on a walking tour of the most interesting and significant sites. The booklet, with its colorful stories and personal histories of early Santa Cruz characters and events, describes gunfights, fortunes made and lost, and stories of abiding love. One of the most striking gravesite monuments is that of Jacob Kron (1823–1879), founder of the A. K. Salz Tannery, known today as the Tannery Arts Center. The statue of a woman, gazing in the direction of the old tannery, tops the tall monument. See if you can find the monument to the 13 young men who died in a devastating explosion at the California Powder Works in April 1898 (See page 83). Other notables buried here include Georgiana Bruce Kirby (1818–1887), an early advocate of civil liberties and women's rights, and Fred Swanton, founder of the Seaside Company and Boardwalk.

■ **Santa Cruz Memorial Park is located at 1927 Ocean Street Extension, Santa Cruz.**

JACOB KRON MONUMENT AT SANTA CRUZ MEMORIAL PARK

40 THE WAX LAST SUPPER

"One of you will betray me," said Jesus to his disciples. Leonardo da Vinci's famous painting, *The Last Supper*, depicts the split second after this dramatic announcement. Using da Vinci's painting as their guide, wax sculpture artists Katherine Stubergh

LIFE-SIZED WAX FIGURES OF JESUS AND HIS DISCIPLES

and her daughter, also named Katherine, completed a life-sized 3-D version of *The Last Supper* in 1950. The figures are now housed at the Santa Cruz Memorial Park. The Stuberghs worked carefully and patiently to make the sculptures as realistic as possible. They placed each hair by hand; this part of the project alone took 8 months to complete. The figures, on display at the Santa Cruz Art League for many years, were acquired by the Santa Cruz Memorial Park in 1990. Over the years, the figures had sustained considerable damage, but the park restored them to their original condition. You can see The Wax Last Supper during the week before Easter, the only time the park makes it available for public viewing.

41 SHROUD OF TURIN REPLICA

On display with The Wax Last Supper is a rare, life-sized replica of the Shroud of Turin. The original Shroud of Turin is a 14-foot-long, ivory-colored linen cloth, believed by some to be the burial cloth placed around the body of Jesus Christ more than 2,000 years ago. It is kept, tightly locked, above the altar of the cathedral in Turin, Italy. If you look closely at this copy, you will be able to see the outline of a body, face and hands. Also on display is a photographic negative of the shroud, which more clearly shows the face and body of the man believed to be Jesus.

PHOTOGRAPHIC NEGATIVE OF THE
SHROUD OF TURIN REPLICA

■ **The Shroud and The Last Supper are located at Santa Cruz Memorial Park & Funeral Home, 1927 Ocean Street Extension, Santa Cruz.**

42 OUR CITY, OUR TOWN TILES

Susana Arias, noted sculptor and painter, is renowned for her environmental awareness and her use of simple and elegant forms. In 1999, she worked on a community project with third graders from local elementary schools to produce a series of 24 large bas-relief tiles. The tiles are mounted onto the outside walls that surround the Santa Cruz Police

Department on Center Street. Eight of the tiles show whimsical landscapes of forest, ocean and beach scenes and 16 tiles celebrate the unique plants and animals of Santa Cruz including dolphins, seals, sandpipers and jellyfish. Not all visits to a police station are fun, but in this case you will marvel at the colorful and creative vision of these young Santa Cruz artists.

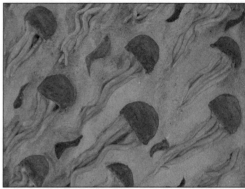

THESE JELLYFISH WON'T STING YOU.

■ **The tiles are located outside the Santa Cruz Police Department, 155 Center Street, Santa Cruz.**

43 TRAFFIC BOX GRAPHICS

At every stoplight there is a signal cabinet housing the computer that controls traffic signals. These large boxes are usually painted gray or green and are designed to fade into the background. But not in Santa Cruz! Since 2002, local artists have transformed dozens of traffic boxes into works of art by painting directly onto the

"HIGH/LOW" BY BRIDGET HENRY

boxes or by using digitally printed vinyl. Some designs are whimsical, some historical and many are just plain beautiful. At the corner of Laurel Street and Pacific Avenue, you will find Vanessa Stafford's four-sided panoramic view of Main Beach including the Wharf, the Boardwalk and sailboats. The traffic box at Front and Cooper Streets is wrapped in a photograph of the original Cooper House. On Seabright Avenue, near Gault School, is a traffic box with two female acrobats flying through the air. Next time you are driving through Santa Cruz, see how many different works of art you can find. It is one time you may not mind waiting at a stoplight.

■ **Traffic box graphics are located all over Santa Cruz City and County.**

44 RIVERBEND PLAZA PARK

A walk or bike ride along the San Lorenzo River below Beach Hill will take you past tiny Riverbend Plaza Park, situated where the river flows through two sharp bends in an area that was once a wide estuarine wetland. The park is designed to evoke the

RIVERBEND PLAZA PARK

river and its history. It is composed of boulders and brick interspersed with grasses. Some of the bricks have words stamped on them. "Channel the River's Energy," reads one. "Flow," reads another. "Front Street Chinatown," "Water Carnival," and "Market Gardens," are on others. There are a few black-and-white photographs affixed to some of the boulders, including a Santa Cruz Water Carnival image from the 1890s and a photo of the great Christmas Flood of 1955.

■ **Riverbend Plaza Park is located at Third Street and Laurel Street Extension on Beach Hill in Santa Cruz.**

45 BEFORE NOW AT DEPOT PARK

Evoking the plants found around the nearby lagoons and marshes of Santa Cruz, eight slender, curving metal stalks grow about 25 feet high from the concrete at Depot Park. The painted aluminum spires change from green to a golden yellow as they rise toward the sun. Created by artist Carolyn Law and erected in 2006, the sculpture, Before Now, also includes a flagstone path interspersed with cut and polished stones. The art is part of a small park with a children's teeter-totter, a kid-powered merry-go-round, a bike park with ramps, and a picnic area. It is located across the parking lot from the soccer fields in Depot Park.

■ **Depot Park is located at 119 Center Street, Santa Cruz.**

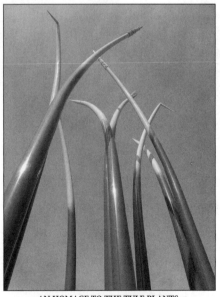

AN HOMAGE TO THE TULE PLANTS
OF NEARY LAGOON

46 MONTEREY CYPRESS

Above the San Lorenzo River, high on Beach Hill and overlooking Downtown Santa Cruz, stands one of the oldest surviving trees in the city. Believed to be close to 200 years old, this enormous Monterey cypress has been a steady presence as Beach Hill has developed from a residential neighborhood of mariners to a resort for tourists. As part of the city's Heritage Tree program, this magnificent tree was commemorated by the Santa Cruz City Council in 1983. Reach the tree from Downtown by climbing the steps from Laurel Street Extension.

TWO-HUNDRED-YEAR-OLD MONTEREY CYPRESS

■ **The tree is located at the intersection of Cliff and Third Streets, Santa Cruz.**

47 CARMELITA COTTAGES

Tucked under gnarled old trees on Beach Hill is a small cluster of tiny Victorian cottages behind a white picket fence. These are the Carmelita Cottages, and they are among the oldest buildings on Beach Hill. The property had 13 owners in

THE ORIGINAL CARMELITA COTTAGE WAS BUILT IN 1872.

its complicated history, including sea captains, gold miners, shop owners, a politician, a barkeeper, jilted wives and widows. Lottie Thompson Sly, its longest inhabitant, finally bequeathed the cottages to the city in a handwritten will in the mid-1950s. Lottie's father, steamer captain Timothy Dane, built the main cottage on the property in

1872, one of six in the complex. The other cottages were either built on the property or moved to this location over the years. Lottie inherited the cottages and lived here most of her life. When she died, she stipulated that the property was to become a park, "cleared and properly landscaped, making it a restful place for the public to enjoy." The property is now a city park and International Youth Hostel.

■ **The Carmelita Cottages are located at 317–321 Main Street, Santa Cruz.**

48 BEACH HILL HISTORIC WALK

A walk on Beach Hill is a tour of the changing identity of Santa Cruz, from maritime and rail transportation center to tourist destination. You'll see this history reflected in the buildings here; from sea captains' cottages and wealthy industrialists' mansions to bungalow courts and mid-century motels. Sea captains lived high on the hill in the mid-1800s where their view of shipping activity in the bay was uninterrupted. Later, when the railroad was extended to Beach Street in 1876, wealthy industrialists built their mansions on what had become fashionable Third Street. In 1915, when the highway was extended from Los Gatos to Santa Cruz, more tourists were able to come for shorter stays and economy motels were built. Stroll along Third Street to see the remaining grand mansions. Notice the large Victorian home at 924 Third Street, with its prominent tower visible from Downtown Santa Cruz. Take a look at the significantly remodeled Victorian at 80 Front Street, now a retirement home. This building was so dilapidated in the 1960s that Alfred Hitchcock used it as his inspiration for the ruined mansion in his movie *Psycho*.

■ **This eclectic neighborhood is located between Third and Beach Streets, and Front and Cliff Streets.**

A REMNANT OF MID-CENTURY TOURISM

GRAND VICTORIAN MANSION AT 417 CLIFF STREET

CHARMING STICK-EASTLAKE AT 1005 THIRD STREET

THE SANTA CRUZ BEACH BOARDWALK

One of the few remaining seaside amusement parks, the Santa Cruz Beach Boardwalk has thrived for over 100 years. A distinctive combination of thrill rides, kiddie rides, arcade games, clothing stores, souvenir shops and unusual foods (deep-fried Twinkies!) keeps it interesting for all ages. Plus, the beach is only a few steps away.

■ **The Boardwalk is located at 400 Beach Street, Santa Cruz.**

49 GIANT DIPPER ROLLER COASTER

If you've been to the Boardwalk, there is a good chance—if you are brave enough—that you've already taken a ride on the Giant Dipper Roller Coaster. You are not alone. It has been ridden more than 60 million times by people from all over the world. Designed by Frank Prior and Frederick Church, and built by Arthur Looff, the wooden Giant Dipper opened on May 17, 1924. It was built in 47 days

for $50,000. One of the oldest roller coasters in the United States, it has been designated as a national historic landmark. Exactly one-half-mile long, the ride lasts one minute and fifty-two seconds, or about a zillion heartbeats. The layout is called a "double out and back" and takes riders racing through curves at speeds of up to 55 mph. The roller coaster's peak is 70 feet high, but you'll swear it is higher. The Giant Dipper has been featured in many films, including *The Lost Boys, Sting II* and *Sudden Impact*. If you want to call yourself a Santa Cruzan, you really should take a ride at least once; but if you don't, there is always the carousel.

A CHAIN LIFT TAKES YOU UP 70 FEET, AND THEN GRAVITY TAKES OVER!

50 LOOFF CAROUSEL

Whether you are a kid enjoying your first merry-go-round, a teenager competing with your friends to grab the metal rings, or an antique buff marveling at the artistry of Charles I. D. Looff, you will want to visit this historic carousel. Installed on the

Boardwalk in 1911, it has 73 horses and two chariots. Each horse is beautifully hand-carved and painted, and no two are the same. Riders on the outer circle of horses can stretch to reach a ring dispenser (one of only a few in the world still in operation), grab a steel ring and try to toss it into the open mouth of a clown to trigger bells and lights. Prized as souvenirs, the Boardwalk replaces 70,000 rings every year. An original 1864 Ruth and Sohn band organ plays music for the ride. The

SEVENTY-ONE LEAPING HORSES REVOLVE AROUND THE HISTORIC LOOFF CAROUSEL; TWO OTHERS JUST STAND.

organ has 342 pipes, a glockenspiel and percussion instruments. Even if you don't want to take a ride, it's worth it to just sit on the nearby benches and watch the horses gallop while you listen to this historic music machine.

51 LAFFING SAL

She is a 5-foot-5-inch redhead with freckles, bad teeth and a nonstop, loud, raucous laugh that is at first surprising, then a bit annoying, but ultimately endearing. Her name is Laffing Sal and her friendly face, waving arms, and big grin greet visitors at the beachside entrance to Neptune's Kingdom on the Santa Cruz Beach Boardwalk. Originally displayed at the Fun House at Playland at the Beach in San Francisco until it closed in 1972, Laffing Sal later stood in obscurity in a small private museum for over 30 years. In 2004, the Boardwalk purchased her at auction for $50,000 and gave her an extensive mechanical and cosmetic makeover.

THIS LADY NEVER STOPS LAUGHING.

Although at one time there were around 300 Laffing Sals at amusement parks around the country, very few remain. She is a rare, 70-year-old icon and you shouldn't miss a chance to hear her famous cackling laugh.

SANTA CRUZ MUNICIPAL WHARF

The 2,745-foot-long Santa Cruz Municipal Wharf was built in 1914 to make it easier to load ships with cargo. Today, the Wharf is one of Santa Cruz's great tourist attractions where you can spend the day fishing, shopping, eating or taking in the view with one of the coin-operated telescopes.

■ **The Santa Cruz Municipal Wharf is located at the corner of Pacific Avenue and Beach Street, Santa Cruz.**

52 IN THE TIDES OF TIME

Near the Santa Cruz Municipal Wharf entrance, you will find a large, multipiece sculpture that looks like an open door with a big ball and several fruitlike wedges scattered around it. This is In the Tides of Time by Irish sculptor Alan Counihan, known for bringing the surrounding landscape and its significance to his pieces. The sculpture is composed of dark limestone and is embedded with small shells. The meaning is perhaps best explained by the artist's poem, inscribed on the sculpture, which begins:

> "In the tides of time
> We have sought
> Safe harbor
> Here
> On this western shore"

■ **To read the rest of the poem, visit the sculpture near the parking lot to the right of the Santa Cruz Municipal Wharf entrance.**

IN THE TIDES OF TIME BY ALAN COUNIHAN, 1995

53 SEA LIONS AT THE WHARF

SEA LION PUPS ON THE WHARF

The best place to watch sea lions up close is at the Santa Cruz Municipal Wharf. Any time of day or night you are certain to see dozens of these animals preening, jostling and nuzzling each other, or just snoozing in the sun. From large ferocious males to small pups, you will find them spread out on boat landings or near the end of the Wharf, lying on the substructure above the water. You may see them leaping out of the water onto the beams, sometimes making several attempts to get there while onlookers cheer them on.

■ **Look for the sea lions on and around the Santa Cruz Municipal Wharf.**

54 MARCELLA FISHING BOAT

Her name is *Marcella,* and she sits on the Santa Cruz Municipal Wharf, her bow pointing out toward Lighthouse Point. A Monterey Clipper fishing boat, the *Marcella* is a memorial to the pioneer commercial fishermen of Monterey Bay. Genoa Boat Works of San Francisco built the 26-foot *Marcella* in 1918, and she was used in the Monterey Bay sardine industry, along with many others like her. Sardine fishing in Monterey Bay peaked in the late 1930s and first half of the 1940s and declined rapidly after that due to overfishing. The *Marcella* was found in the 1960s on the mud flats of Moss Landing. She was eventually restored, and today you can take a close look at the *Marcella* and read more of her story at a nearby kiosk. If you have time, take a stroll to the end of the pier. Be sure to visit the other kiosks along the way that explain the fishing and natural history of Monterey Bay.

■ **You will find the *Marcella* about halfway down the Santa Cruz Municipal Wharf.**

THE *MARCELLA* ON THE SANTA CRUZ MUNICIPAL WHARF

55 LYNCH HOUSE

Overlooking the Boardwalk and the Santa Cruz Municipal Wharf stands one of the most prominent historic homes in Santa Cruz, the gleaming white Lynch House. This Italianate-style home was built in 1877 for Sedgwick Lynch, an early Santa Cruz

THE SEDGWICK LYNCH HOUSE, 1877

builder and gold miner, at a cost of $12,000, an outrageous sum at the time. The house was considered one of the best modern residences in Santa Cruz County, and it was written that from the veranda one could see "a view of the endless panorama of passing sails and ocean steamers far out on the broad Pacific." Early photographs show the house standing alone high on the bluff surrounded by fields. The building was later a hospital, an office and a vacation rental. After a long period of neglect, the once dilapidated home was restored and is now an elegant inn.

■ The Lynch House is located at 174 West Cliff Drive, Santa Cruz.

56 BEARS ON WEST CLIFF DRIVE

Two concrete bears that stand on each side of a West Cliff Drive driveway, overlooking the Wharf and the Boardwalk, have been there for as long as most people can remember. But how did they get there? Rumor has it that two trees once stood where the bears are now. When the trees died, the base of each was carved into the shape of a bear. Finally, even the carvings began to deteriorate and so, in an effort to preserve them, someone applied a concrete covering. They have been like that ever since. Their painted faces are not friendly, but many longtime Santa Cruz residents regard them fondly.

■ You can visit the bears at 170 West Cliff Drive, Santa Cruz.

A LOCAL BROWN BEAR

MONTEREY BAY SANCTUARY EXPLORATION CENTER

Want to experience life under the bay? The Monterey Bay National Marine Sanctuary is like a large national park off the coast of Central California. Larger than Yellowstone National Park, it extends from Marin to Cambria and encompasses more than 6,000 square miles of ocean. This underwater sanctuary includes over 300 species of fish, more than 90 different seabirds and 33 marine mammals. In 2012, the Sanctuary

THE RECLUSIVE AND SCARY-LOOKING WOLF EEL

Foundation opened a two-story Exploration Center with more than 7,000 square feet of exhibit space designed to introduce the public to the extraordinary natural resources of the National Marine Sanctuary. Located near the Santa Cruz Municipal Wharf, this small, admission-free center is full of state-of-the-art video displays describing everything from the geology of the shoreline to the deep-sea rocks and creatures of the 12,713-foot-deep Monterey Submarine Canyon. Visitors can use an interactive multiscreen Google Earth display to view the sanctuary or guide a remotely operated vehicle to explore a replica of a deep-sea canyon. One exhibit area lets you walk below a kelp forest complete with sea animals and divers with animated talking heads. Make sure not to miss the exquisite short film presented in the Exploration Theater where you will see wonderful views of life in and on the bay. Kids can also clamber on a life-sized sculpture of a whale tail in front of the center.

■ **The Monterey Bay Sanctuary Exploration Center is located at the corner of Pacific and Beach Streets in Santa Cruz.**

THE MONTEREY BAY SANCTUARY EXPLORATION CENTER WAS DESIGNED BY THOMAS HACKER ARCHITECTS.

WESTSIDE SANTA CRUZ

From the waves crashing against the cliffs along West Cliff Drive to the terraced neighborhoods below the University of California, the Westside combines great views, beautiful homes and revitalized industrial areas. Highway 1, known as Mission Street through town, divides the lower and upper Westside.

SURFER STATUE

The 18-foot-tall, lifelike bronze statue of a longboard surfer that stands on West Cliff Drive above Steamer Lane "is dedicated to all surfers past, present and future," according to the plaque affixed to its base. The location is fitting, as Steamer Lane is one of the most challenging surfing spots in the world. Unveiled in 1991 during the annual O'Neill Coldwater Classic surfing contest, the statue was created by local sculptor Brian W. Curtis and San Francisco artist Tom Marsh. Members of the Santa Cruz Surfing Club, a group formed in 1936, conceived of the statue and raised the funds for it. Visit the statue and sit on a nearby bench to watch today's surfers ride the waves.

■ **You will find the surfer statue on West Cliff Drive at Pelton Avenue above Steamer Lane, Santa Cruz.**

SURFER STATUE ABOVE STEAMER LANE

59 ■ NEARY LAGOON

Neary Lagoon is a natural wetland believed to have been a bend in the San Lorenzo River that gradually separated from the main river. The native Ohlone people lived for thousands of years in camps surrounding the lagoon. Here they could take advantage of the abundant waterfowl and plant life that they used for food, tools and decoration. Originally 75 acres and extending to Laurel Street and Pacific Avenue, today the lagoon is a 14-acre freshwater marsh, part of a 44-acre wildlife refuge and park. The lagoon is home to migratory and resident birds, and birdwatchers can see ducks, coots, grebes, swallows, herons and many others. The habitat and viewing areas are designed to preserve this

FLOATING BOARDWALKS ON NEARY LAGOON

natural wetland, and you can spend a peaceful hour meandering around the lagoon on a series of floating boardwalks and paths. Dotting the park are benches where you can sit and enjoy the rhythm of this lovely place and interpretive guide signs that inform you about the lagoon and its ecosystem. If you come in the early morning or near dusk, you will be treated to busy bird-feeding activity.

■ **The main entrance to the Neary Lagoon Wildlife Refuge and Park is at 110 California Street near the intersection of Bay Street, Santa Cruz.**

60 ■ BIRD AND ANIMAL TRACKS

Do you want to see what a heron track looks like? Or that of a coot, or a raccoon? At the main entrance to Neary Lagoon is Neary Lagoon Park. You will find tennis courts and picnic tables as well as a sandy playground with play equipment for children. But most fun are the impressions of bird and animal footprints that track across the concrete. Each series of footprints leads to an interpretive sign with information about the animal that made them.

HERON TRACKS

61 MARK ABBOTT MEMORIAL LIGHTHOUSE

"This Mark Abbott Memorial Lighthouse is dedicated to all youth whose ideals are the beacons to the future." So reads the dedication plaque on this quaint red brick lighthouse that was built as a memorial to Mark Abbott, an 18-year-old surfer who

drowned while body surfing at Pleasure Point in 1965. His parents donated the money to build the lighthouse on this site where an old wooden lighthouse had once stood. The new lighthouse was completed in 1967, and Mark Abbott's ashes are interred at the base of the lighthouse tower.

■ **The lighthouse is located on Lighthouse Point on West Cliff Drive, Santa Cruz.**

THE SANTA CRUZ SURFING MUSEUM IS INSIDE.

62 SANTA CRUZ SURFING MUSEUM

Just above Steamer Lane and housed in the Mark Abbott Memorial Lighthouse, you will find the Santa Cruz Surfing Museum. Founded by local surf groups in 1985, this small museum is packed with artifacts and traces the history of surfing in Santa Cruz. From the visiting Hawaiian princes who originally introduced surfing to Santa Cruz in 1885 to the high-tech boards and wetsuits used today, you will get a feel for why locals claim Santa Cruz as the *real* Surf City. Be sure to check out the jagged tooth marks from a 1987 great white shark attack! It might just keep you out of the water.

■ **The Surfing Museum is located in the Mark Abbott Memorial Lighthouse at Lighthouse Point, Santa Cruz.**

THIS LONGBOARD IS MORE THAN 10 FEET LONG AND WEIGHS 95 POUNDS.

63 SAINT JOSEPH MEDITATION PATH

Behind the Shrine of Saint Joseph Catholic Church on West Cliff Drive is a lovely meditation path called The Seven Sorrows and Joys of Saint Joseph. The path winds around 7 two-sided bronze relief panels, each of which depicts a sorrow on one side and a joy on the other. Thomas Marsh, who also co-designed the surfer statue on West Cliff Drive, sculpted the panels. Marsh oriented the panels in such a way that the morning sun shines on the Joys and the afternoon sun on the Sorrows. There are prayer cards available to take with you at the beginning of the short walk, if you wish. After your walk, be sure to visit the neighboring gardens, statuary and grotto.

- The meditation path is located at 544 West Cliff Drive, Santa Cruz.

MEDITATION POINT

64 HISTORIC STREETCAR WHEELS

Did you know that Santa Cruz once had an extensive streetcar system? In 2005, city workers unearthed a set of rusty old streetcar wheels during construction on a Laurel Street water main. They were part of the streetcar system that once connected Santa Cruz and the surrounding areas. The first streetcars in 1875 were horse drawn. During the 1890s the cars were electrified and by 1926, motorized buses had replaced them all. Woodrow Avenue, Cayuga Street and Morrissey Boulevard were among the Santa Cruz streets built with center median strips designed for streetcar tracks. The unearthed streetcar wheels are now part of an informational display at the foot of Woodrow Avenue. As you inspect the display, try to imagine streetcars running down the center median in front of you.

THESE WHEELS WERE EXCAVATED IN 2005.

- The historic streetcar display is located at the intersection of West Cliff Drive and Woodrow Avenue, Santa Cruz.

65 HOUSES ON WEST CLIFF DRIVE

West Cliff Drive stretches along the northern edge of Monterey Bay, passing Steamer Lane, Lighthouse Point and miles of crashing surf. It is also home to multi-million-dollar houses and historic mansions. At the corner of Santa Cruz Avenue is Epworth-by-the-Sea, an Eastlake-style estate built in 1887 with large porches overlooking the Wharf and beautifully landscaped grounds. Next door sits the 1907 Mission Revival Darling House, designed by William H. Weeks and built of solid concrete with a tile roof, copper rain gutters and downspouts, and windows of beveled and leaded glass. One of the most unusual houses along West Cliff is not a fancy mansion at all, but an authentic 1930 log cabin. According to the

THE DARLING HOUSE AT 314 WEST CLIFF DRIVE

Santa Cruz Historic Building Survey, it is thought to be the only one in the City of Santa Cruz. The log cabin house is right across from the cliffside home at Mitchell's Cove where scenes from the Clint Eastwood movie *Sudden Impact* were filmed. In recent years, many modern houses with astounding views have been built along this picturesque drive. The 2.5-mile walk or drive gives you views of both architectural and natural treasures.

■ **West Cliff Drive extends from Bay Street to Natural Bridges State Beach in Santa Cruz.**

66 THE GIANT HEDGE

The hedge on Getchell Street may be one of the largest you have ever seen. It is at least 20 feet tall and 250 feet long, dwarfing cars and people. Stand next to it and try to see the top. You will crane your neck trying. This hedge is made up of densely

THE GIANT HEDGE ON THE WESTSIDE

planted Monterey cypress trees that are pruned to bush form and is at least 100 years old. There is an entryway carved through the greenery to allow access to the home behind it, but this giant hedge is otherwise impenetrable.

■ **Take a detour off West Cliff Drive to see this natural wall located at 221 Getchell Street, Santa Cruz.**

NATURAL BRIDGES STATE BEACH

The 65-acre Natural Bridges State Beach, at the northernmost end of the Monterey Bay, offers a wide variety of sights including its famous natural bridge, the Monarch Butterfly Preserve, tide pools, meadows full of spring wildflowers and the picturesque Moore Creek. There is a picnic area, a visitor center and a bookstore.

■ **The main entrance is located at the end of West Cliff Drive with a walk-in entrance off Delaware Avenue in Santa Cruz.**

---

67 MONARCH BUTTERFLY PRESERVE

The vivid orange-and-black monarch butterfly is beautiful and always fun to spot, but what if you could see thousands of them at once? Every fall, usually starting in mid-October, monarch butterflies begin arriving on their annual migration to the Central Coast for the winter. One of their favorite places to stop is the Monarch Butterfly Preserve at Natural Bridges State Beach. At the end of a 200-yard-long, gently sloping boardwalk, the preserve viewing area contains a grove of eucalyptus trees that are sheltered from the wind. From fall to early spring, thousands (and sometimes tens of thousands) of monarch butterflies can be seen hanging in giant clusters from the trees. On warmer days (when the temperature is above 55 degrees), you can see them flying about searching for nectar and water; in January and February you can watch their mating rituals. These beautiful winged tourists fly up to 2,000 miles to winter here in Santa Cruz and each year a new generation (the great-great-grandchildren of the previous year's butterflies) arrives. Take a visit to the preserve to welcome them.

■ **The Monarch Butterfly Preserve is located within the park across from the visitor center.**

VIEW THE BUTTERFLIES ON YOUR OWN OR SIGN UP FOR A DOCENT-LED TOUR.

THE REMAINING ARCH AT NATURAL BRIDGES

Millions of years ago, pounding waves at the northern edge of Monterey Bay carved three arches out of a mudstone bluff that jutted into the sea. Those arches became part of what is now Natural Bridges State Beach. Over the years, erosion from the waves undercut the arches. In the early 1900s, the outermost arch fell into the sea, leaving offshore rocks known as sea stacks; in 1980 the innermost arch broke during a storm. Now just the middle arch remains. Take a stroll onto the beach for a close-up view of the waves surging through the archway. Although the remaining arch looks sturdy, its opening will continue to expand until someday it too will succumb to the power of the sea. While you are at Natural Bridges State Beach, especially if you visit at low tide, you will also want to check out the large expanse of tide pools to see sea urchins, sea stars and hermit crabs. The parking area just outside the park, in front of the entrance station at the end of West Cliff Drive, is a great place to look for gray whales between December and April during their annual migration to and from the Baja Peninsula.

■ **The remaining arch is best viewed from the beach within Natural Bridges State Beach.**

THE LAST REMAINING ARCH AT NATURAL BRIDGES STATE BEACH SITS ALONE IN THE SURF.

SEYMOUR MARINE DISCOVERY CENTER

A great destination for both locals and tourists, the Seymour Marine Discovery Center presents indoor and outdoor educational exhibits, a small aquarium with a touch tank, and the Ocean Discovery Shop. The Seymour Center is the science education center for Long Marine Laboratory and the docents are highly knowledgeable and very enthusiastic. The Seymour Center is the final building on the ocean bluff within the UC Santa Cruz Marine Science Campus.

■ **The Seymour Center is located at 100 Shaffer Road, at the end of Delaware Avenue in Santa Cruz.**

---

69 BLUE WHALE SKELETON

The gigantic, sun-washed blue whale skeleton, outdoors next to the Seymour Center, is one of the most impressive natural history sights you will ever see. At 87 feet long, "Ms. Blue" (as she is called by volunteers at the center) is one of only four blue whale skeletons in the United States and likely the largest in the world. The jawbones alone are 18 feet in length. Estimated to have been about 50 years old, she washed ashore

at Fiddler's Cove near Pescadero in September 1979. She was buried by UCSC biologists and allowed to decompose. In 1985 her bones were unearthed, and local geologist Frank Perry was hired to clean and mount them on a steel framework. In 1999, Ms. Blue was moved to the

STAND NEXT TO MS. BLUE TO APPRECIATE HOW HUGE SHE IS.

Seymour Center. Under the guidance of UCSC veterinarian Dr. Dave Casper, she was refurbished and her 60 missing bones were re-created. Inside the Seymour Center is a display that provides an up-close view of one of her vertebrae and an X-ray image of how her giant flipper might have looked.

70 MAST OF THE SHIPWRECKED LA FELIZ

Sticking up above the cliffs just behind the Seymour Center is a tall wooden mast. In October 1924, the schooner *La Feliz*, heading from Monterey to San Francisco with a cargo of canned sardines, crashed against the rocks just beyond the present-day Natural Bridges State Beach. All 13 people on board, plus a dog and a cat, were rescued with the help of local farmers and residents. Ask a Seymour Center docent to tell you the detailed story of the rescue and the recovery of the cargo and equipment.

THE RESTING PLACE OF THE SHIPWRECKED *LA FELIZ*

71 ELEPHANT SEAL SCULPTURES

If you visit the Seymour Center, don't miss the three life-sized sculptures of a female elephant seal, her pup and a rearing bull elephant seal. They reside just in front of the center. Made out of fiberglass and polyester resin with exacting attention to detail, the seals look and feel extremely lifelike. Unveiled in 2004 to honor Long Marine Lab volunteers, the sculptures were fabricated by David Caldwell from molds borrowed from the California Academy of Sciences. In the late 1980s, the Academy hired a team of six artists to work with elephant seal experts to create clay sculptures in order to make the original latex molds. They are amazing works of art. If you go to Año Nuevo State Reserve at the right time of the year, you can see actual living elephant seals, but you will never get this close.

ADULT MALE NORTHERN ELEPHANT SEALS
CAN WEIGH UP TO 5,000 POUNDS.

72 ■ KITCHEN'S TEMPLE

In the 1930s, an eccentric brickmason named Kenneth Kitchen built one of the most unusual structures in Santa Cruz. Surrounded by a low handmade wall of curving concrete, perfectly aligned bricks and inlaid abalone shells, is a series of brick buildings and minaret towers called Kitchen's Temple. These structures are intricately detailed with sparkling mosaics. Even from the street, the detail of the inset shells is

CELESTIAL SYMBOLS DECORATE THE TEMPLE ENTRY.

fascinating. If you visit, look closely at the triangular top of the entryway, which is decorated with celestial symbols. Having spent time in Turkey during World War I, Kitchen was inspired by religious buildings he saw there. The first structure he built on his property was the pump house. During World War II, he added a radio tower to the top. He is said to have spent night after night outdoors lying on a mattress wearing headphones, convinced he could hear German submarines off the Santa Cruz coast. Today, privately owned, the temple is surrounded by unkempt palm trees. A No Trespassing sign hangs from a chain at the entrance.

■ **Kitchen's Temple is located at 519 Fair Street, Santa Cruz.**

THE ENTRANCE TO KENNETH KITCHEN'S TEMPLE

SMALL CREATURES

THESE LITTLE CREATURES WILL WIN OVER YOUR HEART.

If you want to see a perfect example of a Santa Cruz treasure hidden in plain sight, locate the traffic island that separates the one-way residential portion of Trescony Avenue from the commercial section of the street next to the Mission Street McDonald's. Peering up at you from inside the triangular island are the eyes of dozens of small creatures. These tiny, colorful ceramic sculptures were created by local elementary school students under the direction of artist and sculptor Susana Arias. In an area of about 25 square feet, interlaced with sculpted fallen leaves, are bunnies, ladybugs, salamanders, a skunk, a mama bird sitting with her eggs, earthworms, and many other little animals and insects. You'll have to bend over to look closely, but the more you look the more you will see. The site is well worn, and over the years some of the sculptures have been damaged, but it is a wonderful example of the extensive array of public art that can be seen all over the county.

■ **Small Creatures is located in the traffic island across from 247 Trescony Street, east of Mission Street, in Santa Cruz.**

CHECK OUT THIS TRAFFIC ISLAND FULL OF TINY, WHIMSICAL ANIMALS.

WESTLAKE PARK

Tucked in an upper Westside Santa Cruz neighborhood is the small, spring-fed, man-made lake and park known as Westlake Park. This lush landscape is a lovely spot for both people and birdlife. Hundreds of ducks, geese and various other bird species make this

REDWOOD TREES AT WESTLAKE PARK

lake their home. A large tule grass island is a natural bird habitat at one end of the water. The lake is usually stocked with fish and if you are 16 years old or younger, or 65 or older, you are permitted to fish here. There is a lovely stand of tall redwood trees along one edge of the water and behind the trees is a green playing field where neighbors play games of soccer. At one end of the park is a children's playground with play equipment including swings, slides, and a large sand area.

■ **Westlake Park is on Bradley Drive off Spring Street, Santa Cruz.**

75 HOME OF PEACE CEMETERY

Known as *Beit Shalom* (Home of Peace), this small Jewish cemetery on the west side of Santa Cruz is a rustic and peaceful place to visit. Santa Cruz pioneer Moses Meder (a non-Jew) gave or sold the land to the Jewish community for the establishment of the cemetery in 1877, on condition that his family could be buried there. You will find the Meder family plot at the back of the cemetery surrounded by large old

THE CEMETERY HAS BEAUTIFUL GRAVE MONUMENTS.

trees and lovely grave monuments, both old and new. In accordance with Jewish law, the cemetery which is part of the Temple Beth El community is closed from dusk on Friday night to dusk on Saturday night.

■ **The cemetery is located at 425 Meder Street, near Western Drive in Santa Cruz.**

ANTONELLI POND

Created in 1908, when Moore Creek was dammed as a log pond for the San Vicente Lumber Company's sawmill, Antonelli Pond today is a destination for hiking, birdwatching, fishing or simply enjoying the beauty of this quiet place. The 6.4-acre pond is home to many species, including a wide range of birds such as egrets, ducks and geese. Deer, raccoon and coyote also forage here. Especially good times to spot wildlife are in the early mornings and late afternoons when you may find yourself joined by neighborhood dog walkers and joggers. Wooden platforms at water's edge are prime spots for fishing. A hiking trail circles most of the pond. If you add a brief walk on the railroad trestle at the north end of the pond, you will be able to walk the entire perimeter. The San Vicente Company originally called the pond Moore Creek Lake and Mill Lake. Later, the Antonelli Brothers owned the pond and surrounding land, which they used for begonia cultivation. Antonelli Pond is owned and managed by the Land Trust of Santa Cruz County.

■ **Antonelli Pond is located across from Natural Bridges State Beach at 2360 Delaware Avenue, Santa Cruz.**

ANTONELLI POND IS A GREAT PLACE FOR HIKING, BIRDWATCHING AND FISHING.

UC SANTA CRUZ

UCSC was founded in 1965. Made up of 10 colleges spread over 2,000 historic and beautiful acres of rolling hills and forest, the university is full of artistic, historic and natural wonders. Its main entrance is at Bay and High Streets and the west entrance is on Empire Grade Road.

THE PORTER WAVE

On the hillside overlooking Monterey Bay, near the entrance to Porter College on the campus of the University of California, Santa Cruz, sits the iconic Porter Wave, also known as The Squiggle and The Flying IUD. Officially untitled, it was created by artist, sculptor and former UCSC student Kenny Farrell as a senior project in 1974. Stretching about 20 feet wide and 9 feet high, the red-orange steel structure is a favorite hangout for students, who can often be seen sitting or lying on the sculpture enjoying the expansive views. Clamber on top and join them.

■ **The sculpture is located at Porter College, UCSC.**

THE PORTER WAVE IS A GREAT PLACE TO WATCH THE SUNSET.

COWELL LIME WORKS HISTORIC DISTRICT

Lime was a key element of the mortar, plaster and whitewash used to construct California buildings during the state's rapid growth after the Gold Rush. The weathered limestone and wooden buildings at the main entrance to the UCSC campus are the remains of what was once the largest lime manufacturing operation in California. Today, you can visit 30 acres of surviving structures including limekilns, the cooperage, the paymaster's house and many other buildings that were designated as the Cowell Lime Works Historic District in 2008. In 1865, Henry Cowell acquired an interest in the lime works that had been operating here since 1850. He eventually became the sole proprietor and owned all the land where UCSC is now located. Lime operations continued at this location until around 1920.

■ **Pick up a walking tour guide at the Main Entrance Kiosk, near the intersection of Bay and High Streets, Santa Cruz.**

78 THE LIMEKILNS

Henry Cowell used the groves of redwood trees that grew on his land to fuel large kilns that you can still see today. The kilns were loaded with limestone from above and with redwood through the openings below. Fires were set and burned for about 3 days, with temperatures reaching as high as 1,700 degrees. The heat would convert the limestone to lime, which would then cool for 2 days before being loaded into barrels at the nearby cooperage.

HISTORIC MACHINERY UNDER THE COOPERAGE AND THE LIMEKILNS BEYOND

79 THE COOPERAGE

Barrels for shipping lime to market were made in the cooperage. You will notice that the cooperage was built so wagons could pull in under the building to be easily loaded for shipment. From here, the barrels were taken by ox-driven carts down Bay Street (known then as Lime Kiln Road) to Cowell Wharf and loaded onto large steamships for transport up and down the California coast. The east end of the building was removed in 1965 to make way for Coolidge Drive.

THE COOPERAGE WAS BUILT AFTER THE ORIGINAL BUILDING WAS
DESTROYED BY FIRE IN 1869.

80 THE STONEHOUSE

Now known as the stonehouse, this solid-looking building was the paymaster's house. For many years, Henry Cowell paid his men only once each year for their hard work. Payroll would be brought down from San Francisco, guarded overnight in the stonehouse and paid to workers the following day. Later, Cowell paid his workers once each month and the stonehouse became the ranch commissary, where employees could purchase supplies.

THE STONEHOUSE NEAR HIGH STREET

81 ALAN CHADWICK GARDEN

In 1967, English master gardener Alan Chadwick was invited to come to the newly opened UCSC campus to help establish a student garden and apprentice-training program. The result was one of the first organic gardens in California. Chadwick, an innovative leader of organic farming techniques, created his own

BEEHIVES AT ALAN CHADWICK GARDEN

gardening style by combining biodynamic agriculture (which uses organic methods, microorganisms and lunar cycles), with the French intensive gardening method in which plants are placed closely together to retain moisture and reduce weed growth. Today, you can visit this lush 2-acre site that is crammed full of a seemingly

ALAN CHADWICK GARDEN HAS MANY SPECIES OF FRUIT TREES.

impossible number of fruit trees. The many varieties of apple, pear and citrus trees, as well as flowers and vegetables, are marked with shiny labels noting the type of each plant. In the spring, bees from several brightly colored hives buzz steadily from tree to tree. The garden is a part of the Center for Agroecology & Sustainable Food Systems, a training and research program, and you will most likely see students working in the garden while you are there.

■ **Alan Chadwick Garden is located on the UCSC campus, below Merrill College.**

THE FARM

Following the success and popularity of Alan Chadwick Garden, the 25-acre UCSC Farm was founded in 1972 on grasslands that were part of the original Cowell Ranch. Today, the Farm includes hand-worked beds of annual and perennial food and ornamental crops, mechanically cultivated row crops, orchards and research plots. The agroecology laboratory, a solar greenhouse and a visitor center serve as research, teaching and training facilities. Like the Alan Chadwick Garden, the UCSC Farm is part of the Center for Agroecology & Sustainable Food Systems. The center's mission is to "research, develop, and advance sustainable food and agricultural systems that are environmentally sound, economically viable, socially responsible, nonexploitative, and that serve as a foundation for future generations." Workshops are available to the public on subjects ranging from organic gardening, seed starting and fruit tree pruning to beekeeping and raising chickens and ducks. If you are interested in gardening, your visits to the Alan Chadwick Garden and the Farm will be inspirational and educational at any time of year. Both are open to the public. Look for the Farm's informative, self-guided tour brochure, available at the entrance.

■ **The UCSC Farm is located off Coolidge Drive, near the main entrance to the UCSC campus.**

STUDENTS WORKING AT THE UCSC FARM

GRATEFUL DEAD ARCHIVES

Honor the Dead, and stay for much more. The UCSC Library Special Collections now houses the Grateful Dead Archives, an astounding collection of musical and historical artifacts including posters, cover art, photographs and other memorabilia documenting the great jam band from its founding in 1965 (the same year UCSC was born) to the present. The collection also includes stage props, backdrops, awards and a complete set of Grateful Dead recordings. The Dead Archives are part of the UCSC Library Special Collections. Since the late 1960s, Special Collections has been preserving and promoting a vast and fascinating collection of historical documents. Among them are the country's largest holding of Edward Weston photographs, the archives of science fiction writer Robert Heinlein, Santa Cruziana artifacts, along with hundreds of rare fine press and artist books, many by local presses.

PUT ON YOUR TIE-DYE AND HEAD UP TO UCSC.

■ **The Grateful Dead Archives are located in the newly remodeled McHenry Library on the UCSC campus.**

84 5,000 BUTTERFLIES

To see an extraordinary assortment of preserved insects, plants and animals, you'll want to visit the UCSC Museum of Natural History Collections. Established in 1994 with a focus on the flora and fauna of UCSC and the Central Coast, the museum contains more than 90,000 items. It houses 400 reptile specimens, study skins of 900 mammals and 1,200 birds, and a large collection of local fungi. The insect

BUTTERFLIES ARE JUST A SMALL PART OF THE MUSEUM'S COLLECTIONS.

collection includes the world-class Gerhard Ringel Butterfly Collection. The late UCSC math professor traveled the world collecting mostly tropical butterflies, many of which he hand-raised from eggs or caterpillars to create perfect, undamaged specimens. Five thousand butterflies and moths are displayed in glass cases, exhibiting astounding variations in color, design and size. Since the butterflies and all the museum's collections are organized for research use, they can only be viewed by the public at special open house events or by appointment. For more information about how to view these treasures, search the web for the UCSC Museum of Natural History Collections. It is worth the extra effort.

■ **The collections are located in the Natural Sciences 2 building, UCSC.**

85 PENDLETON MINERALS COLLECTION

Hidden away on Science Hill at UCSC is an extensive mineral collection donated to the university in 1986 by Norman and Gertrude Pendleton. Eight glass cases display classic and unusual examples of minerals from around the world. There are more than

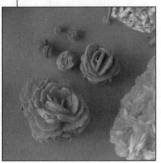

350 different mineral samples organized by type, including a large separate collection of over 100 California minerals reflecting the diverse character of the state's geology. As you read the commentary within the displays, you will learn about sulfides, oxides, borates, carbonates and other minerals, in addition to getting a mini-introduction to geology. One especially interesting and beautiful display showcases a dozen large and unusual examples of crystalline minerals, including the rare black crystals of neptunite, the intense pure-blue crystals of linarite and the delicate milky-white radiating sprays of mesolite.

CHECK OUT THE BARITE "ROSES."

■ The Pendleton Minerals Collection is located in the corner of the large lobby area of the Earth and Marine Sciences building on the UCSC campus.

86 ELOISE PICKARD SMITH GALLERY

Located at Cowell College, the Eloise Pickard Smith Gallery was the first art gallery on the UCSC campus. Founded in 1966 by Eloise Smith, wife of Cowell Provost Page Smith, the gallery focuses on art of the Monterey Bay Region, with occasional special exhibitions focusing on subjects related to the college. The gallery, which hosts about six exhibitions during the year, consists of two exhibit spaces totaling approximately 750 square feet. It is open October through May when classes are in session. In the passageway near the inside entrance to the gallery are the John Dizikes Art Cases.

In the early '80s, Provost Dizikes decided the college should also showcase student artwork. This mini-gallery is run by students, with thematic displays usually featuring two artists at a time.

■ The Eloise Pickard Smith Gallery and the Dizikes Cases are located next to the Cowell College Dining Hall entrance, UCSC.

THE GALLERY OPENED JUST A YEAR AFTER THE FOUNDING OF UCSC.

87 MARY PORTER SESNON ART GALLERY

THE SESNON GALLERY IS OPEN YEAR-ROUND,
TUESDAY THROUGH SATURDAY.

It is no surprise that one of the most respected art galleries in the county is located at art-centric Porter College on the UCSC campus. Established with a 1968 donation by Barbara Sesnon Cartan in memory of her mother, the Mary Porter Sesnon Art Gallery hosts national and international exhibitions of contemporary art in the 1,000-square-foot space. The gallery's goal is to "encourage interdisciplinary discourse through the lens of the arts." Over the course of each academic year, the gallery has put on four to five exhibitions, including the "Irwin Scholars," an annual scholarship exhibition showcasing the works of undergraduate UCSC students who have shown proven excellence in the arts. The Sesnon Art Gallery also organizes public lectures, symposia, and other programs to provide curricular support to the campus art community. Within the same building complex is the Porter College Faculty Gallery that presents work by both campus and visiting art faculty.

■ **The Mary Porter Sesnon Art Gallery is located in Porter College on the west side of the UCSC campus.**

88 PORTER TOTEM POLE

In 1984, under the direction of art professor Doyle Foreman and sculptor Georganna Malloff, UCSC students and staff carved the 42-foot-high Tree of Life totem pole that now stands at Porter College. The sculpture depicts animals from the earth, sea and sky including a dolphin, a hungry coyote, a coiled snake, horses, humans, a crocodile and gracing the top, a heron with wings spread wide. The word *totem* comes from a First People's term for clan, or kinship, and the plaque at its base states that this totem pole "represents a powerful statement of individuals who worked together to create a unified statement about their humanity and the beauty around them." Beautifully carved and weathered with age, it is worth a close and contemplative look.

CREATURES HUMAN AND ANIMAL
GRACE THIS TOTEM.

■ **The Porter totem pole is located in front of Residence Hall A on the Porter College campus.**

89 EMPIRE CAVE

Cave Gulch, behind Porter and Kresge Colleges on the UCSC campus, is known for a series of caves formed by acidic groundwater percolating along faults and fractures through underground marble. Empire Cave, known on campus as Porter Cave, is one of the most accessible of the caves and a popular student destination despite early efforts by the university to discourage visitors. To enter the

THIS LADDER TAKES YOU INTO THE FIRST CHAMBER OF EMPIRE CAVE.

cave, you descend a 20-foot steel ladder through a ragged hole in the concrete block that covers the entrance. At the bottom, you will be standing in a large chamber (approximately 20 by 30 feet). To the right and behind the ladder is the entrance to a second large chamber. You will need to crouch and clamber about 30 feet down a slick path before you get to a high-ceilinged area where you can stand and use your flashlight to view the cave walls. Although the cave is geologically unremarkable, you can see a few stalactites and stalagmites. To get to a third small chamber, you need to go up and to the left and crawl on your hands and knees. Empire Cave can be very muddy and, if students have been partying, you'll sometimes see beer cans and other litter. The cave is cool, the air is moist and it can be very quiet. Caving can

THE MULTIPLE CHAMBERS ARE COOL, DARK AND MUDDY.
NEVER GO CAVING ALONE.

be risky, but if you choose to visit, bring at least two headlamps or flashlights per person, wear clothes you don't mind getting muddy and don't go alone. Be careful: all of the cave, including the ladder, can be very slippery. To get to the caves, follow the path behind Porter College down across Porter Meadow. The path will enter the trees and then head to the right paralleling Empire Grade Road. After about 50 yards, you will come to a graffiti-covered concrete block on the right with the opening on the top.

■ **Empire Cave is located behind Porter College at UCSC.**

90 BANANA SLUGS

Although it is beyond the purview of this book to discuss the diversity of flora and fauna in this great county, we have to mention the banana slug. Usually bright yellow (hence the name), slimy and with two sets of tentacles, they grow to almost 10 inches long. They like the damp of the redwood forest and are inveterate

recyclers, processing leaves and dead plant material. Banana slugs can be spotted on the UCSC campus and are especially prevalent in nearby Henry Cowell State Park. In the early years of UCSC, partly as a statement against the overly competitive nature of college sports, the banana slug became the unofficial mascot for the campus. In 1986, after years of resistance and controversy, the administration finally made the banana slug the official UCSC mascot. When walking our local redwood forests, look carefully to

THE BANANA SLUG IS THE OFFICIAL UCSC MASCOT.

see if you can find this famous mascot out for a stroll. A banana slug's top speed is about 6.5 inches per minute, so you will have plenty of time to check it out.

■ **Banana slugs are found on the forest floor, especially in cooler, darker spots or on tree trunks.**

91 TREE NINE

On the upper campus of UCSC stands the famous Tree Nine. It is a 103-foot-tall Douglas fir with spiraling branches that, for decades, was a popular and beloved climbing spot. Due to safety concerns, in 2010 the University removed the branches from the first 25 feet to discourage climbing. Before the limbs were cut, if you were brave and/or foolish enough to climb to the top, you could see panoramic views of Monterey Bay. (Search YouTube to see these views.) While there are multiple creative reasons why it is called Tree Nine, the most likely explanation is that it was originally the ninth stop on the UCSC Natural Reserve Seep Zone Interpretive Trail. Although no longer accessible to climb, this tree is a well-known part of campus lore.

■ **Tree Nine is located behind Colleges Nine & Ten in the middle of the UCSC Natural Reserve.**

TREE NINE IS EQUAL IN HEIGHT TO A 10-STORY BUILDING.

HUMMINGBIRD TRAIL AT THE UCSC ARBORETUM

The best place in Santa Cruz to see hummingbirds performing their aerial acrobatics is on the quarter-mile Hummingbird Trail at the UCSC Arboretum. On this trail there are numerous nectar-producing plants, such as showy Grevillea, Erica and Salvia, which attract these tiny iridescent birds. In the spring, you may see male birds zoom to heights of 75 to 100 feet, pause and then dive down over desirable females, only to pull up at the last second with a sharp squeak. This is all part of their unique mating dance. Anna's hummingbirds are year-round residents and Allen's hummingbirds begin arriving in February and stay through summer. The Hummingbird Trail is only one of the many paths you can follow at the 80-acre arboretum, the collection point for more than 10,000 rare, endangered and unusual plants from around the world. There are also gardens dedicated to California natives, cacti and succulents, rare fruiting plants, aromatic plants, a eucalyptus grove and a kauri forest. The arboretum's Hummingbird Days festival is held on a spring weekend every year and features special programs for adults and children that include hummingbird tours, slide shows, lectures, and arts and crafts.

A PATH LEADING TO THE HUMMINGBIRD TRAIL

■ **The UCSC Arboretum is located at 1156 High Street, Santa Cruz.**

SAN LORENZO VALLEY & SCOTTS VALLEY

This area is comprised of the historic San Lorenzo Valley lumber towns of Felton, Boulder Creek and Ben Lomond along Highway 9, and Scotts Valley on Highway 17. Dense forests and stunning river and mountain views characterize this region. There are also remnants of the once active lumber and lime industries, as well as a few quirky tourist attractions.

THE CHIMNEY TREE

"They are ambassadors from another time," wrote John Steinbeck about the *Sequoia sempervirens*, commonly known as coast redwoods. *Sempervirens* is Latin for evergreen. These amazing trees have been growing for thousands of years, and sometimes reach heights of more than 300 feet. In 1902, the conservationist Sempervirens Club achieved their first goal of preserving these ancient giants with the opening of Big Basin Redwoods State Park, which was the first state park in California. One of the most popular short hikes in the park is the six-tenths of a mile Redwood Trail near the visitor center, where you can stroll beneath these giants. Don't miss one of the most fascinating trees on the walk, the Chimney Tree, hollow from its base to the top. Enter the tree through a jagged fire scar and look up. Incredibly, you will see a small circle of blue sky high above you. It is believed that a number of fires from long ago ignited the tree's heartwood, eventually burning a hollow from top to bottom. Amazingly, the tree still lives, evidence of the strength and durability of these magnificent treasures.

■ **The Chimney Tree is on Redwood Trail, located in Big Basin Redwoods State Park.**

THE CHIMNEY TREE IN BIG BASIN REDWOODS STATE PARK

PARADISE PARK – HISTORIC SITE OF CALIFORNIA POWDER WORKS

Paradise Park is just that, a little slice of residential paradise just 2 miles outside the City of Santa Cruz. Founded in 1924 by a group of Freemasons from Fresno as a camping getaway from the Central Valley's summer heat, Paradise Park is today a private community of tiny cottages built alongside the San Lorenzo River. The site is also the original location of the California Powder Works (1861–1914), the first and largest gunpowder manufacturer on the West Coast. The powder works was originally established to supply local gunpowder needs during the Civil War, when shipments from the East were stopped out of fear that Union gunpowder would be stolen by Confederate raiders. Today, you can visit the remnants of the powder works by taking a self-guided walking tour. Check in at the park office on Keystone Way for directions or to purchase a walking tour booklet (with maps) for a small fee. Placards at key sites in Paradise Park also explain the history of the area. While you are in the office, take a look at the motorized model of the powder-making process and the collection of local artifacts, including the 100-pound cannon shells that were fired into the surrounding hillsides to test the gunpowder!

■ **The entrance to Paradise Park is located on Highway 9, about 2 miles north of Downtown Santa Cruz.**

PARADISE PARK ENTRANCE ON HIGHWAY 9

95 THE POWDER HOUSE

The Powder House is now a private residence but was originally built in 1865 for an entirely different purpose. It was used as a storehouse for gunpowder, with as many as 30,000 kegs kept here at a time. Naturally, the danger of explosion was great and

THE POWDER HOUSE IS NOW A PRIVATE RESIDENCE.

the Powder House was built for that possibility. The building is 25 by 110 feet, and the walls are 14 inches thick. The wooden floor was put together with wooden dowels instead of nails to avoid sparks, and the floor rests on a 3-foot granite foundation. The roof was made of corrugated sheet metal, intended to give way in an explosion and direct blasts upward and away from people and other buildings. In 1898, a series of huge explosions did occur at the California Powder Works, killing 13 men and boys, and injuring 25. It was the deadliest explosion in the 50-year history of the business and just a year later, the county declared the area unsafe for employee housing.

■ **The Powder House is located at 132 Keystone Way in Paradise Park.**

96 POWDER WORKS COVERED BRIDGE

The Powder Works Covered Bridge is the only covered bridge in Santa Cruz County still in active use by both cars and pedestrians. It was built in 1872 after the original

bridge over the San Lorenzo River washed away. A replacement was needed quickly, so Bernard Peyton, superintendent of the California Powder Works sprang into action. He contacted the Pacific Bridge Company in San Francisco, whose slogan was "Built by the mile, cut and sold by the yard." The company had a patented design of pre-cut and finished bridge kits, which could be quickly and economically assembled on site. The Powder Works Covered Bridge took only 71 days from contract to completion and cost just $5,250.

■ **Take the scenic path along the river to the bridge from the Paradise Park Office on Keystone Way.**

COVERED BRIDGE BUILT IN 1872

ZIPPING THROUGH REDWOODS

Next time, instead of taking a walk through the redwoods, consider flying. The Redwood Canopy Tour at Mount Hermon in Felton has created a zipline course through the redwoods that allows you to soar above Bean Creek Canyon at heights of up to 150 feet. (That is 15 stories high!) Six ziplines and two rope bridges stretch between circular platforms

FROM A PLATFORM 140 FEET HIGH, SOARING ALONG 300 FEET OF CABLE

built high up in the redwoods. The ziplines range in length from 130 to 440 feet. The tour equips you with helmets, gloves and safety harnesses, gives you training and makes sure everything is safe, but it's up to you to step off the platform. The exhilarating rides are a little scary at first, but you will quickly get into the "hang" of it. The 2-hour tour is led by friendly and experienced guides who, in addition to keeping everyone safe and calm, share their knowledge of redwood forest ecology. Tour groups are limited to eight at a time and prepaid reservations are required. The zipline is a unique way to further appreciate our beautiful redwood forests.

■ **The Redwood Canopy Tour is located at Mount Hermon Christian Conference Center, 37 Conference Drive, off Graham Hill Road in Felton.**

EVEN ON THIS 150-FOOT BRIDGE, YOU ARE ATTACHED TO A SAFETY LINE.

ROARING CAMP AND BIG TREES RAILROAD

Roaring Camp (named for the wild settlement established by mountain man Isaac Graham in the 1830s) is designed to give the feel of going back in time to the pioneer days. To enter Roaring Camp, you walk across a replica of a 19th-century covered bridge and meander down a path toward a general store, sheriff's office and an old-fashioned depot. But it's the train rides that bring people here. The first railroad began carrying tourists to Big Trees Grove (now Henry Cowell Redwoods State Park) and to the beach in Santa Cruz from San Jose in 1875. Today you can take the beach train through the state park, down the San Lorenzo River Gorge, and through a tunnel built in 1875 to the Santa Cruz Beach Boardwalk. Or you can ride an authentic 100-year-old steam train on a narrow-gauge railway up the steep mountainside through redwood forests and across trestles. The camp area itself is free, but there is a charge for train rides. Call ahead for the train schedule and fees. If you go, you will be experiencing an important part of Santa Cruz Mountains history.

■ **Roaring Camp is located off Graham Hill Road about one-half mile south of Felton.**

LOCOMOTIVE #1, *DIXIANA*, BUILT IN 1912, IS READY TO TAKE PASSENGERS UP THE MOUNTAIN.

FELTON COVERED BRIDGE

Just off Highway 9 is the old entryway to the town of Felton, the Felton Covered Bridge. The 180-foot bridge spans the San Lorenzo River and is one of two remaining covered bridges in Santa Cruz County. The other is the Powder Works Covered Bridge a few miles downstream, in Paradise Park (see page 83). The Felton Covered Bridge is believed to be the tallest covered bridge in the United States, but no one really knows why it was designed that way. In 1982, the structure was badly damaged during heavy winter rainstorms. It was fully restored in 1987 using original materials and local builders. Today you can walk through the bridge, your footsteps echoing off the wooden planks. Take a peek out of one of the several openings to see the meandering river below. At one end of the bridge is the large grassy Covered Bridge Park. There are several picnic tables and a children's playground. At the other end is a picturesque equestrian center.

■ **The Felton Covered Bridge is located at the intersection of Mt. Hermon and Graham Hill Roads, in Felton.**

THE FELTON COVERED BRIDGE WAS THE ONLY ENTRY TO FELTON FOR MANY YEARS.

LOCH LOMOND

If you want the experience of a mountain lake without having to drive to the Sierra, visit Loch Lomond Reservoir. Called the jewel of the Santa Cruz Mountains, this reservoir sits surrounded by steep redwood forest. On sunny days, the union of the deep green trees and the shimmering blue water is stunning. Created by the construction of the 195-foot-tall Newell Creek Dam in 1962, the reservoir is 3 miles long and one-quarter mile wide with an average depth of about 100 feet. Managed by the City of Santa Cruz, the Loch Lomond Recreation Area offers a rental fleet of pedal boats, rowboats and electric-assist boats. There is also fishing for largemouth bass and bluegill, and 10 miles of scenic hiking trails. Since Loch Lomond is a drinking water reservoir, you cannot swim or use powerboats. With a capacity of 2.8 billion gallons, it is a critical summer water source for the City of Santa Cruz. As a natural reserve, Loch Lomond is also home to many small animals and birds, including osprey and the western pond turtle, which are both considered species of special concern. This recreation area is a great place to come to spend a quiet and lazy afternoon relaxing in a boat on the reservoir or hanging out in one of the many picnic areas. The reservoir is open daily March through Labor Day and weekends-only through mid-October. You can find Loch Lomond by carefully following the signs after turning off Graham Hill Road near Felton onto East Zayante Road.

■ **Loch Lomond is located about 30 minutes north of Santa Cruz near the mountain community of Lompico.**

IT ORIGINALLY TOOK 2 YEARS TO FILL THIS 2.8-BILLION-GALLON RESERVOIR.

HENRY COWELL REDWOODS STATE PARK

The scenic and serene Henry Cowell Redwoods State Park comprises 1,750 acres in lower Felton plus an additional 2,390 acres in the northern Fall Creek section of the park. The main park has more than 15 miles of hiking trails, old-growth redwoods and forest stands of fir, oak, madrone and ponderosa pine.

■ **The park is located on Highway 9 just south of Felton.**

101 THE FREMONT TREE AND THE GIANT

The Redwood Grove Nature Trail in Henry Cowell Redwoods State Park is a short (eight-tenths of a mile) loop through a magnificent 40-acre grove of original growth coastal redwoods. The self-guided loop takes you past two especially interesting sights: The Fremont Tree and The Giant. On February 25, 1846, while on a surveying expedition in California, Lieutenant John C. Fremont purportedly camped in the hollow of a huge redwood tree. Today, you can clamber inside the Fremont Tree through a small opening and stand in the very same chamber that Lt. Fremont did more than 150 years ago. While in the grove, Fremont also identified and measured a 350-foot-tall redwood that is now known as The Giant. It is 17 feet wide and about five times as tall as the Santa Cruz Town Clock. Unfortunately, having twice lost its top during storms, it is now "only" 270 feet tall, the third tallest in the park. (The tallest tree is 277 feet and stands behind the visitor center, unmarked.) The path to The Giant allows you to see it standing alone as you approach, making it easy to appreciate its impressive size and bulk. This grove of redwoods has been visited by presidents and other famous dignitaries and is an easy stroll for youngsters and oldsters alike.

PRESIDENTS W. H. HARRISON AND TEDDY ROOSEVELT CAME TO SEE THESE REDWOODS.

■ **The entrance to the loop is near the park's visitor center.**

102 2,200-YEAR-OLD REDWOOD

THIS TREE WAS MORE THAN 2,200 YEARS OLD.

In front of the Henry Cowell Redwoods State Park visitor center is a 9-foot cross section of one of the oldest known coast redwood trees. It was harvested in 1934 in Humboldt County in the area now known as the Avenue of the Giants. Growth rings indicate that the tree was over 2,200 years old when it was felled, dating its beginning to the second century BC. Read the growth ring labels for a quick lesson on the history of the world, starting from the birth of Jesus through the founding of Big Basin State Park in 1902.

■ **Located in front of the visitor center.**

103 OBSERVATION DECK

For 360-degree views of the Santa Cruz Mountains and (on a clear day) a nice view of Monterey Bay, head up to the Observation Deck. It is a wood and concrete structure built at the highest point in Henry Cowell State Park. The hike to the Observation Deck from the campground area of the park takes about 15 to 20 minutes. The trail is very sandy—this area was once part of an ancient seafloor and scientists

YOU MAY SEE HORSES USING THE SPECIAL DRINKING FOUNTAINS NEXT TO THE DECK.

have found marine fossils here, such as shark teeth and sand dollars.

■ **Located at the intersection of Pine Trail and Ridge Fire Road.**

104 THE OVERLOOK BENCH

For another magnificent view, hike up to the San Lorenzo River Overlook bench. To the left you will see the ridgeline and thick forest that divides Henry Cowell Redwoods State Park from UCSC. Down in the valley, you will see glimpses of the river, the meadows of Pogonip and the City of Santa Cruz. And just beyond, weather permitting, you will see the white framework of the Giant Dipper roller coaster and the mouth of the San Lorenzo River.

■ **Located 1.6 miles up the Pipeline Road Trail starting from the Graham Hill Road turnout at the southeast edge of the park.**

VIEW THE SAN LORENZO WATERSHED.

BIGFOOT DISCOVERY MUSEUM

On a wall-sized Santa Cruz County map, in this tiny two-room museum near Henry Cowell Redwoods State Park, are pushpins representing the many local sightings of Bigfoot, the large, hairy apelike creature also known as Sasquatch. Michael Rugg founded the museum in 2003 and has compiled a huge and fascinating collection of Bigfoot reference materials, artifacts and memorabilia. While most mainstream scientists dismiss the evidence of this controversial hominoid, many people are true believers and Rugg keeps an open mind. The display at the entrance to the museum describes the history of Bigfoot and shows a historical timeline of sightings over the centuries. Bigfoot in Popular Culture is a large collection of comics, stuffed toys, soaps, action figures, playing cards and even Bigfoot Beer. Across the top of one wall are tabloid newspaper headlines of Bigfoot sightings. The second room has monitors playing video clips of Bigfoot encounters, plaster casts of footprints and scat, as well as comparative models of the skulls of apes and early humans. The museum also houses a collection of art and music featuring Bigfoot. As you wander through the Museum, you will be treated to Bigfoot-themed songs playing on the stereo. The museum is hard to miss. As you drive down Highway 9, a few hundred yards past the main entrance to Henry Cowell Redwoods State Park, you will see a 10-foot-tall carved wooden statue of Bigfoot, carrying a baby Bigfoot on its shoulders. Stop by to say hello.

■ **The Bigfoot Discovery Museum is located at 5497 Highway 9, Felton.**

THIS BIGFOOT LIVES IN THE FOREST NEAR FELTON.

106 FALL CREEK LIMEKILNS AND BARREL MILL SITE

There are many remnants in Santa Cruz County of the once extensive lime industry that existed here in the late 1800s and early 1900s. One of the largest of these operations was the Fall Creek site of the IXL Lime Company located in today's Fall Creek State Park. Henry Cowell later purchased the company and made it part of his extensive Cowell Lime and Cement Company (See the Cowell Lime Works Historic District description on page 70.) During its peak years, this site produced more than one-third of the lime in Santa Cruz County, including much of the lime used in the cement to rebuild San Francisco after the 1906 earthquake. Today you can take a shady, 1.3-mile hike along Fall Creek, through second-growth redwoods and Douglas fir, to see the moss-covered ruins of this once thriving operation. An additional 1.5-mile walk along an old wagon road and creekside trail will lead you to the barrel mill site. Machinery used to make the barrels still remains scattered there.

■ **Hike to the site via Fall Creek Trail, in Fall Creek State Park, 1400 Felton Empire Road, Felton.**

THE RUINS OF THE FALL CREEK LIMEKILNS

107 QUAIL HOLLOW RANCH

In 1937, Laurence Lane, publisher of *Sunset* magazine for 62 years, purchased the 300-acre Quail Hollow Ranch outside of Felton. The farmhouse had been built in the late 1860s, but Lane had his own ideas about how he and his family would live on this beautiful property. Many of the concepts of *Sunset*, then aptly subtitled "The Magazine of Western Living," such as indoor/outdoor living and the open kitchen floor plan, were first tried here. Now a Santa Cruz County park, you can visit this rustic estate and trace its evolution from early farmhouse to incubator of Western living. Today, the house is the park's visitor center and the Lane's former living room exhibits a variety of mounted birds and wild animals native to the area. The large kitchen is still used for food preparation, especially for groups attending scheduled classes and workshops about the natural and cultural history of the area. The horse stables the Lanes remodeled are still in use, and you can explore the property via the 4.5 miles of hiking trails that wind through a variety of habitats including pond, riparian, chaparral, sand and evergreen. Don't miss this beautiful spot.

■ **Quail Hollow Ranch is located at 800 Quail Hollow Road, Felton.**

THE VISITOR CENTER AT QUAIL HOLLOW RANCH

FELTON HOTEL MURAL

High on the wall of one of Felton's oldest buildings, the former Felton Hotel, is a mural that shows the town's most important structures from the late 1800s to 1950. The mural was commissioned by Frances Taber, the building's current owner, as a tribute to her late uncle, Nick Belardi, who once ran the 22-room hotel and bar on this site. Muralist William Northcutt painted the mural, taking 3 years to complete the job. The Felton Hotel is shown as it appeared in the 1930s, with Frances, her family and her uncle Nick standing on the front porch. Also in the mural are the Felton Covered Bridge and the town's first gas station. The Felton Library is included in the mural because Nick Belardi bought the building when it was a church and donated it to be used as a library in honor of his deceased first wife, Faye Belardi. The shared memories, stories and photos of many of Felton's residents and passers-by contributed to the mural's creation. The artwork's finishing touch was the tribute from a devoted niece: "In Loving Memory of Nick Belardi, Original Owner of the Felton Hotel."

■ **The Felton Hotel mural is located at the intersection of Felton Empire Road and Highway 9, Felton.**

THE FELTON HOTEL AS IT APPEARED IN THE 1930s

109 HOWDEN CASTLE

Ben Lomond might seem an unlikely place to find a medieval castle, but Howden Castle has been standing above the banks of the San Lorenzo River, just off Highway 9, since 1927. Robert Howden built this fanciful estate, modeled on the castles of

THE CASTLE OVERLOOKS THE SAN LORENZO RIVER.

his native Scotland. The stone castle, overlooking the river and a small beach, has numerous towers and five balconies with parapets, some decorated with heraldic imagery. The building is brightly painted in pinks and browns and the glass windows depict Scottish scenes and the poems of Sir Walter Scott and Robert Burns. On one side of the building, a tromp l'oeil princess peers out of a window. Surrounded by trees, the castle's location is beautiful.

■ **You will have the best views of Howden Castle on Highway 9 from the bridge over the San Lorenzo River, at the north end of Ben Lomond.**

110 SANTA CRUZ MOUNTAINS ART CENTER

You can't miss the Santa Cruz Mountains Art Center, with its cheerful facade decorated by a brightly colored abstract design. In changing exhibits, this gallery showcases a wide variety of handmade arts and crafts by local artists. Exhibitions include paintings, jewelry, ceramics, glasswork, woodwork, basketry, textiles and more. The center offers adult, teen and children's classes in a range of subjects, and also sponsors after-school art classes in drawing, painting, sculpting, and handbuilding with clay in local schools. Visit the gallery shop where you can purchase the work of local artists.

THE EXUBERANTLY DECORATED ART CENTER

■ **Santa Cruz Mountains Art Center is located at 9341 Mill Street, Ben Lomond.**

111 ST. ANDREW'S CHURCH

A visit to St. Andrew's Episcopal Church in Ben Lomond is like being in a fairy tale. This small, red, Gothic-style church, which seats only 120 worshippers, stands in a picturesque setting on a quarter-acre site, under a large old redwood tree. The church

was named after the patron saint of Scotland and has been serving locals and visitors to the area since its construction in 1899. The interior of the church is as charming as its exterior. Like the entire building, it is made of native redwood. Most of the colorful stained glass windows were made by local artists. Over the years, many of the furnishings have been handmade by parishioners including the impressive pipe organ, the needlepoint seat cushions in the chancel, and the choir stall. The overall effect is one of coziness and warmth.

■ St. Andrew's Church is located at 101 Riverside Avenue, Ben Lomond.

THE CHURCH WAS CONSECRATED IN 1901.

112 ST. ANDREW'S CHURCH ORGAN

When you enter St. Andrew's Church, the fantastic pipe organ immediately commands your attention. This grand instrument sits high on the wall above the church entrance. It was specially built and installed in 1960 by chemistry and physics teacher Preston Boomer with the help of his high school students, and by Bill Reid, a professional organ builder. In 1973 it was enlarged from its original three ranks of pipes to seven ranks. Boomer, a longtime teacher at San Lorenzo Valley High School, spent the inheritance from his grandfather to buy the organ pipes. You can see and hear the St. Andrew's organ during church services. Learn more by visiting the church website.

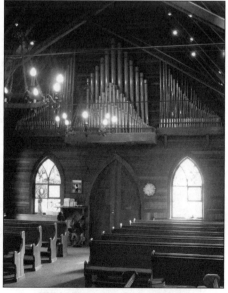

PIPE ORGAN AND CHURCH INTERIOR

THE OLD ALBA SCHOOLHOUSE

Above Ben Lomond and surrounded by dense redwoods stands the old Alba School, the last remaining one-room schoolhouse in Santa Cruz County. Your first view of this quaint red schoolhouse will make you feel as if you are in a different time. The community built this charming building with its distinctive bell tower in 1895. A second room was later built onto the back of the school using material from the dismantled Sequoia School, which had been located outside Boulder Creek. Mountain children attended Alba School until it was closed in 1941, and the schoolhouse became a library and community center. For a time, the bell mysteriously disappeared from the tower. Years later, it was found and restored to its rightful location. Today the school is used for community gatherings such as the annual Fourth of July celebration, which has been taking place reliably for more than 118 years. Everyone is invited to this fundraiser that celebrates our nation's founding with a flag raising, hot dogs, hamburgers and patriotic songs. Guided tours of the schoolhouse include a modest museum with a display of school furnishings, old photographs and school diplomas.

■ **Alba School is located 2 miles up Alba Road from Highway 9, Ben Lomond.**

ALBA SCHOOL AND THE RESTORED BELL IN THE TOWER

114 SAN LORENZO VALLEY MUSEUM

The former Grace Episcopal Church is a simple but beautiful Gothic Revival–style building, now home to the San Lorenzo Valley Museum. The building was built in 1906 and, according to museum staff, may have been constructed from a single redwood tree. Life in the San Lorenzo Valley logging community was rough, and drinking and carousing were a way of life. In the early 1900s, the clash between those who wanted to restrict liquor, gambling and prostitution, and those who didn't, became increasingly aggressive. In the conflict, arsonists destroyed the Methodist and Presbyterian churches, but Grace Episcopal

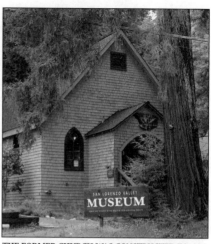

THE FORMER CHURCH WAS CONSTRUCTED IN 1906.

Church survived and is today the oldest church building in Boulder Creek. You can visit during museum hours and see permanent and rotating exhibitions of the history of the San Lorenzo Valley. There is an extensive logging exhibit including a steam-operated drag saw and numerous logging implements. There is also a fully equipped kitchen circa 1900, with a large collection of early kitchen utensils and appliances.

■ **The San Lorenzo Valley Museum is located at 12547 Highway 9, Boulder Creek.**

115 THE MOUNTAIN ECHO LEAVES

For many years, the *Mountain Echo* newspaper was the voice of San Lorenzo Valley. The paper was founded in 1896 by C. C. Rodgers and later run by his brother, W. S. Rodgers. In 1914, W. S. Rodgers leased the *Mountain Echo* to Luther McQuesten. Unable to collect money he was owed by subscribers and advertisers,

THE *MOUNTAIN ECHO* PRINTED ON A LEAF

McQuesten soon found himself in dire financial straits. In desperation and unable to afford newsprint, McQuesten printed the November 11 and November 18, 1916, issues of the *Mountain Echo* on large cottonwood leaves. Several of these remarkable editions survive today, and you can ask to see them at the San Lorenzo Valley Museum.

■ **The San Lorenzo Valley Museum is located at 12547 Highway 9, Boulder Creek.**

Deep within Big Basin Redwoods State Park is the almost 70-foot-high Berry Creek Falls, considered one of the finest waterfalls of the California Coast Ranges. In a beautiful setting surrounded by redwood forest, the wide, shallow falls drop sharply down a steep cliff into a small pool. A viewing platform with a bench where you can take photos and eat a picnic lunch sits about 25 yards from the base of the falls. You can also take the steep trail around the waterfall to get overhead views of the falling water. Starting about one-half mile above the falls are the smaller Silver,

NAMED AFTER TILFORD GEORGE BERRY, A LUMBERMAN AND HERMIT WHO HAD A CABIN AT THE FALLS IN THE MID-1800s

Golden and Cascade Falls. To enjoy the beauty of Berry Creek Falls, however, you have to be prepared for some serious hiking: the minimum round trip is 10 miles and 4 to 5 hours of sometimes-strenuous up-and-down hiking. Trails to Berry Creek Falls can be accessed either near the Park Headquarters in Big Basin Redwoods State Park on Highway 236 north of Boulder Creek or from the trailhead on Highway 1 north of Santa Cruz, across from Waddell Beach. Make sure you pick up a good map, especially if starting from Big Basin, since the trails and multiple routes can be confusing. Mountain bikes are allowed on the lower portion of the trail up from Waddell Beach along the fire road. Both routes offer scenic views, multiple creek crossings (usually, but not always, on seasonal bridges) and opportunities to see wildlife. If you are in good shape and have the time, the hike to Berry Creek Falls is a worthwhile adventure.

■ **Berry Creek Falls is located in Big Basin Redwoods State Park.**

117 GOAT ROCK

Castle Rock State Park sits on the crest of the Santa Cruz Mountains right on the dividing line between Santa Cruz and Santa Clara Counties. This rugged 5,200-acre park, with 35 miles of trails, is famous for its unusual honeycomb rock formations. The namesake Castle Rock is the highest point in the park at 3,214 feet (only a few feet lower than the nearby Mt. Bielawski, the highest point in Santa Cruz County at 3,231 feet). While Castle Rock is worth a visit, the trail to the equally impressive Goat Rock offers stunning vistas south across the entire San Lorenzo Valley to the Pacific Ocean. On a clear day, you can see not only the undulating hills of the Coast Range but also the curving sweep of Monterey Bay. Goat Rock is an impressive sandstone outcropping, honeycombed with small caverns. It is very popular with both rock climbers and hikers who want to take in the panoramic views. According to Don Clark in his book *Santa Cruz County Place Names*, Goat Rock got its name from an early settler whose goats "seemed to like to hang out on the rock." Goat Rock is 1 mile from the trailhead at the main Castle Rock parking area. It is a moderate hike with some short sections of scrambling required. En route, you can take a short side trip to Castle Rock. Perched on the highest ridge in the county, the park is well worth a visit.

■ **The main entrance to Castle Rock State Park is located on Highway 35, 2.5 miles south of Highway 9 and a little less than an hour from Santa Cruz.**

CLIMBERS ENJOY THE HONEYCOMB FORMATIONS AT GOAT ROCK.

118 SCOTT HOUSE

If you'd like to see how Scotts Valley's namesake, Hiram Scott, lived after he settled here, you can visit the house he built. Scott was a true California pioneer. He was a sailor who jumped ship in Monterey; a gold miner who made a small fortune in the mines; and a very successful businessman. He was so successful that in 1850, he paid some $25,000 to buy the Rancho San Agustin land grant, site of present-day Scotts Valley, where he planned to raise horses and grow hay and potatoes. Scott arranged for his family in Maine to join him, and in 1852 and 1853, he built this home. The New England–style Greek Revival house is a small cozy structure composed of a parlor, two bedrooms, a dining room and a kitchen. It is mostly furnished with pieces from the period during which Scott lived in it. The house originally sat on old Los Gatos–Santa Cruz Highway (today's Scotts Valley Drive) but was moved in 1936 to its present location. Since then the camellia tree at the front porch has grown so large, it seems as if the house has always been on this spot. Scott and his family held onto the property until 1872, after which the house passed through at least 19 owners. You can view the interior of the house by arranging a tour with the Scotts Valley Cultural Preservation Commission, or you can peek through the windows to enjoy this unique piece of Scotts Valley history.

■ **The Scott House is located at 1 Civic Center Drive, Scotts Valley.**

THE HISTORIC SCOTT HOUSE WAS BUILT BY HIRAM SCOTT IN 1852–1853.

119 LIFE-SIZED GRIZZLY BEARS AND GIANT MUSHROOMS

ONE OF TWO LIFE-SIZED GRIZZLIES

In the middle of MacDorsa Park, situated behind the Scotts Valley Civic Center, stand two ferocious life-sized grizzly bears facing each other and ready to do battle. They were originally part of a roadside attraction called Lost World that grew out of the famous Tree Circus in Scotts Valley. Lost World displayed these fiberglass bears along with dinosaurs and other creatures, some of which could be seen from Highway 17. After Lost World went out of business, the bears appeared in the Scotts Valley Day parades of the '70s and '80s. If you come to see the bears, you should also check out the two gigantic mushrooms (one more than 8 feet across) salvaged from the Santa's Village amusement park that operated in Scotts Valley from 1956 until 1979.

■ **MacDorsa Park is at 77 Civic Center Drive, Scotts Valley.**

120 PREHISTORIC ARTIFACTS

Scotts Valley is the location of one of the oldest archaeological sites in North America and one of only a few sites where native peoples lived in the same spot for over 10,000 years. A series of excavations in the 1980s (where the current Scotts Valley City Hall now stands) uncovered thousands of stone artifacts dated as early as 12,000 years ago. In the reception area of the city hall, you will find a large glass display case housing stone tools including spear points, hammerstones, drillpoints, and a rare and very old artifact known as an eccentric crescent. An eccentric crescent is a multinotched, bifacially flaked stone object whose function is still unknown. The glass display case

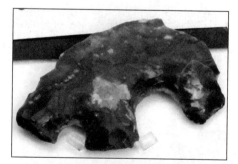

A RARE ECCENTRIC CRESCENT

includes photos of the excavations and detailed descriptions of the artifacts and the significance of the findings. This display is worth a visit if you enjoy archaeology and want to stand where our prehistoric ancestors stood thousands of years ago.

■ **Scotts Valley City Hall is located at 1 Civic Center Drive, off of Hwy 17.**

121 CAMP EVERS FISHING PARK

Tucked in the trees, below busy Mt. Hermon Road, is Camp Evers Fishing Park. It's a tiny 1-acre park designed for young people ages 15 and under. You will know you have found the place when you see the large wood carving of a steelhead trout on the lawn, at the park entrance. This sculpture is part trout and part redwood tree, with the bark of the tree twisting like rough water over the fish's back. The park is stocked with native steelhead and the fishing is free from May to September. If you are lucky enough to catch your limit, enjoy your fresh trout cooked on one of the nearby barbeques.

STEELHEAD TROUT CARVING
AT THE ENTRANCE

■ **Camp Evers Fishing Park is located about one-half mile from Mt. Hermon Road on Glen Canyon Road, Scotts Valley.**

122 LODATO PARK LOOP TRAIL

Just minutes from busy Highway 17 is a hidden woodland get-away: the 50-acre Lodato Park. The park's Loop Trail begins not far from the trailhead, where you will instantly find yourself passing through redwood trees and fern-draped hillsides. Highway 17 and Scotts Valley traffic noise is soon replaced by birdcalls and the peace and quiet of the forest. The trail is a meandering ascent, sometimes winding and narrow. You will see evidence of a long ago fire and logging. At the top of the trail, before you head back down through scrub oaks and aromatic bay trees, you will have a brief view of the hills and Scotts Valley below. You may encounter joggers and walkers from nearby neighborhoods and businesses, but the trail is mostly quiet. The approximately 1.5-mile hike can be easily done in under an hour.

LODATO PARK LOOP TRAILHEAD

■ **The Lodato Park Loop Trail trailhead is located at the rear of the parking lot behind 1800 Green Hills Road, Scotts Valley.**

123 MOTORSPORTS MUSEUM

If you are a race car enthusiast or just someone who can appreciate powerful, beautiful and expensive engineering marvels, you will want to stop by the Canepa Motorsports Museum in Scotts Valley. It is an eclectic collection of more than 20 race cars and about eight motorcycles, with an emphasis on cars from the 1960s through the 1980s, including Formula One, NASCAR, dirt track Sprint Cars and Le Mans winners. Many were owned by famous race car drivers: Richard Petty's bright blue 1969 Ford Torino Cobra is on display, along with Dan Gurney's 1969 500-horsepower Boss 302 Mustang. You can see a number of rare and powerful Porsches, including the last Porsche 935 produced by the Porsche factory and raced by Bruce Canepa himself. Many of the cars have large displays describing their history and racing records. One particularly unusual model is the world's fastest extreme gravity racer (the high-tech version of soapbox derby cars). This space-age pod, designed by Volvo in 2005, holds the gravity speed record of 67 miles per hour. The museum is free and open Monday to Saturday.

■ **The Motorsports Museum is located on the second floor of the Canepa Design building at 4900 Scotts Valley Drive, Scotts Valley.**

THE 1969 PORSCHE IN THE FOREGROUND WON THE 1970 DAYTONA 24 HOURS.

124 TREE CIRCUS

A unique roadside attraction in Scotts Valley during the late 1940s to the early 1960s was the now legendary Tree Circus. Here visitors could see some 70 trees that a farmer named Axel Erlandson had manipulated into unusual shapes using grafting, bending and pruning techniques. Only three trees from this popular outdoor attraction remain in their original location on Scotts Valley Drive and you can see them there today. Erlandson was a bean farmer in the San Joaquin Valley when he noticed that two sycamore trees on his farm had fused and grown together naturally. He began to experiment, and soon Erlandson was training trees into all manner of curious shapes: zigzags, spirals, hearts, ladders and more. In the mid-1940s, Erlandson purchased three-quarters of an acre on the major thoroughfare in Scotts Valley leading to Santa Cruz's beaches. He soon put up a sign, "SEE THE WORLD'S STRANGEST TREES HERE," and charged 25 cents for entry. The outdoor park was featured in *Life* magazine and in "Ripley's Believe It Or Not!" newspaper column. Twenty-nine of the trees were later relocated to Gilroy Gardens Family Theme Park

and put on display. But a three-legged tree and two trees formed as an arch still survive and can be seen at the Scotts Valley location where they were first planted. There is also an exhibit of the Tree Circus at the Museum of Art and History in Downtown Santa Cruz (see page 21).

■ **The original Tree Circus property is currently the site of several businesses and a café located at 4652 Scotts Valley Drive, Scotts Valley.**

TWO REMAINING TREE CIRCUS TREES FORM AN ARCH.

125 THE LAST BILLBOARD

It is not really a destination, although if you are a local, chances are you have seen it hundreds of times. But the billboard on Highway 17 just north of Scotts Valley is memorable because it is the last of its breed. Beginning in the mid-'60s, city officials in Santa Cruz began lobbying for much stronger sign ordinances, including the eventual removal of all billboards; but it did not happen quickly. In the early '80s, a Santa Cruz group calling itself T.I.A. for "Truth In Advertising" took a different approach and began altering the messages on existing billboards. A suntan lotion ad that showed a bikini-clad woman and tiger under the banner "Tropical Blend. The Savage Tan," was changed to "Typical Blend. Sex in Ads" (with the tiger saying "Ah, Meat!"). "Triumph [cigarettes] Taste the Umph" was changed to read "Triumph for Democracy! US out of El Salvador." T.I.A. became notorious, with stories in *Mother Jones* magazine and in the *Los Angeles Times* and other newspapers. Finally in 1986, after years of legal battles, the Foster and Kleiser sign company took down all 21 billboards remaining in town. Well, almost all. It was not until 1995 that the 8-by-16-foot Mystery Spot sign, on Soquel Avenue near Capitola Road, was finally removed. With federal legislation, all billboards along Highway 17 and Highway 1 south to Watsonville also disappeared. However, the billboard on Highway 17 did not go away. It had been there so long that it predated any federal legislation and was allowed to remain. So the next time you drive by that billboard, remember that although it may not be "as lovely as a tree," it is indeed a rarity.

■ **The Last Billboard is located at 7260 Highway 17.**

OUR LOCAL BANK UNDERSTANDS THE VALUE OF THIS RARITY.

THE NORTH COAST

The North Coast of Santa Cruz County offers a rugged coastline with numerous beaches, unparalleled ocean views and many historic buildings. It includes the communities of Davenport, Swanton and within a short drive, the forested hills of Bonny Doon. The North Coast extends about 18 miles from the Santa Cruz city limits along Highway 1 to the San Mateo County line.

126 KITE SURFERS AT WADDELL BEACH

Want a chance to see dozens of surfers pulled by the wind and moving at high speeds through the water while turning, jumping and sometimes soaring into the air? One of the nation's premier kite surfing locations is Waddell Creek State Beach on the windswept north coast of Santa Cruz County. Kite surfers ride short boards and use giant colorful kites, ranging in size from 4 to more than 20 square meters, to propel them across waves and water. One of the biggest attractions, for both the surfer and the viewing public, is "controlled flying." Skilled kite surfers, using waves as launch pads, can sometimes fly 25 or more feet into the air and stay airborne for up to 5 or 10 seconds, performing tricks as they soar above the water. Waddell Beach is a large crescent-shaped beach with consistent and predictable winds. The beach and the adjacent parking lot both provide good viewing areas and although the action tends to be just offshore, having a good pair of binoculars is a plus. While kite surfing happens year-round, the windy season lasts from April to October. When the conditions are right, you will see a spectacular show.

■ **Waddell Creek State Beach is located along Highway 1 just south of the Santa Mateo County line.**

WADDELL BEACH IS KNOWN WORLDWIDE FOR ITS IDEAL WIND AND WAVE CONDITIONS.

WILDER RANCH: HISTORIC COASTAL DAIRY FARM

Six generations of the Wilder family lived on this coastal ranch beginning in 1871, operating their dairy business, and later a cattle and horse ranch. Today, you can visit the ranch grounds and buildings, which have been faithfully preserved as they were before the Wilders sold the property in 1969. In 1972, developers announced plans to construct an extensive residential and commercial development on the site of the 4,000-acre ranch, but a passionate grassroots movement prevented that from happening. Wilder Ranch became a state park consisting of the ranch buildings and 34 acres of hiking, biking and equestrian trails. Led by a costumed docent, you can tour the ranch to see a historic adobe, two Victorian homes, barns, workshops, stables, farm equipment and farm animals. There is also an interpretive center and a well-stocked bookstore that specializes in local and natural history.

■ **Wilder Ranch State Park is located on Highway 1, about 2 miles north of Santa Cruz.**

127 WILDER RANCH HOUSES

Two Victorian ranch houses reveal what domestic life was like while generations of the Wilder family lived here. When you visit Wilder Ranch, you may tour both homes. The older home was built in the 1850s and the house next door was built in 1897. The living quarters in the 1850 home are furnished from that period but, in the 1930s, the kitchen and dining room were significantly enlarged in order to feed ranch employees. In this house, right off the kitchen, you can also see the spartan accommodations of the Chinese ranch cook. The kitchen in the 1897 home is a family kitchen with a large wood-burning stove, pantry and numerous kitchen tools. The rest of this home is furnished as it would have been in the 1930s and '40s. Be sure to notice the fireplace in the parlor, which features an inlaid tile portrait of President McKinley, who was evidently much admired by the Wilders.

WILDER RANCH HOUSE, 1897

128 PELTON WHEEL

PELTON WHEEL IN THE WORKSHOP

The Wilder family implemented many innovative practices while managing their dairy and ranch operations. One of the most inspired was the use of waterpower and a water turbine called a Pelton wheel to run many mechanical devices used on the ranch. In the 1890s, D. D. Wilder constructed a dam 210 feet above his creamery. From there, water was conducted through a pipe to a Pelton wheel, creating enough energy to produce up to 100 horsepower. Later, the Wilders connected their Pelton wheels to electric generators, enabling their ranch to be the first rural ranch in Santa Cruz County to have electric lighting. The main Pelton wheel was lost when the creamery burned down, but several smaller ones survive including one that, through a web of belts, shafts and wheels, still drives machinery in the shop. You can watch a demonstration of the Pelton wheel in the ranch workshop.

129 BLACKSMITH SHOP

Right next door to the Pelton wheel is the ranch blacksmith shop where you can watch a forging demonstration. This is where horses were shod and farm implements made and repaired.

FORGING DEMONSTRATION

130 BOLCOFF ADOBE

If you get excited about early California history, take a close look at the Bolcoff Adobe while you are at Wilder Ranch. The exact origins of the adobe have been lost to history but it is believed José Antonio Bolcoff constructed it between 1830 and 1840. Bolcoff was a Russian whaler who jumped ship in Monterey and married into the prominent Castro family.

BOLCOFF ADOBE

The Castros owned this land as part of the land grant known as Rancho Refugio. The adobe is built almost entirely from adobe blocks made from onsite soil. Many of the roof tiles have been replaced, but some of the handmade tiles left are believed to have come from Mission Santa Cruz. Only remnants of the original mud plaster coating and whitewash remain.

131 FERN GROTTO

Old Cove Landing Trail at Wilder Ranch State Park winds through a Brussels sprout field to the bluffs overlooking the bay. At the Wilder Ranch visitor center, you can pick up a trail guide that highlights plants and animals of the region, as well as its geology. Points of interest are numbered, and when you arrive at Number 8, you will see a very large cave in the distance. This is Fern Grotto and it is worth the climb down to the beach to explore. Because of its sheltered and shady location, many different kinds of ferns thrive here. If you stand at the mouth of the grotto, you will notice water dripping from the roof of the cave. This is believed to be natural seepage through the permeable rock layers and provides a perfect environment for the ferns growing here. If you dare, you can go deeper into the cave or just stand at its mouth and gaze into the darkness.

■ Fern Grotto is off Old Cove Landing Trail, located at Wilder Ranch State Park, 2 miles north of Santa Cruz.

FERN GROTTO IN WILDER RANCH STATE PARK

NORTH COAST RAMPARTS AND TUNNELS

In 1906, the Ocean Shore Electric Railway, in a never-to-be-realized dream to connect Santa Cruz and San Francisco by railroad, built a series of wooden train trestles across stream valleys up the coast toward Davenport Landing. They then dumped earth and rock off the trestles to create a string of massive and level embankments along the coast. Also known as ramparts, they are 36 feet wide at the top—wide enough to accommodate up to three train tracks. From the ocean side, the ramparts are quite recognizable, but as you drive up the coast from Santa Cruz along Highway 1 you may not notice them at first, until you begin to realize that the massive mounds that obstruct your view of the ocean seem surprisingly straight and flat. Controversial at the time they were built, they blocked access to many beaches and lagoons and required the rerouting of coastal streams, including

SAN VICENTE TUNNEL EXITING ONTO DAVENPORT BEACH

San Vicente, Laguna, Liddell and Yellow Bank Creeks. To allow the streams to flow to the sea, tunnels were built through mudstone bedrock on the north side of each trestle rampart, and they can still be seen today. One of the most accessible is the San Vicente Tunnel where the creek empties onto Davenport Beach. It can easily be seen with a short walk down from the parking area directly across from the town of Davenport.

■ **Davenport Beach is located on Highway 1, about 12 miles north of Santa Cruz.**

DAVENPORT

Davenport is a small coastal town just north of Santa Cruz. Beginning in 1905, it became home to a thriving cement manufacturing business when eastern cement entrepreneur William J. Dingee started the Santa Cruz Lime Company on the banks of San Vicente Creek. In 1906, the Santa Cruz Portland Cement Company took over, installed a large cement plant, and the town grew up around the plant. Davenport suffered cataclysmic fires several times in its history and many of the original wooden buildings were burned. With cement being readily available and impervious to fire, two buildings were constructed from poured concrete: the St. Vincent de Paul Catholic Church and the Davenport Jail. They are among the oldest structures remaining in town.

■ **Davenport is located 12 miles north of Santa Cruz on Highway 1.**

---

133 THE CONCRETE CHURCH

The St. Vincent de Paul Catholic Church in Davenport was "poured" in 1915. It was designed by L. Moretti, who modeled the building after a church in his native town of Cevio, Switzerland. The cement used to construct the building was donated by the local cement plant. The church was dedicated on May 16, 1915, with the Holy Cross Choir from Santa Cruz and the Santa Cruz High School Band on hand for the occasion. The small church, which sits on a bluff above the town, is still in use today.

■ **St. Vincent de Paul Catholic Church is located at 123 Marine View Avenue in Davenport.**

THE ST. VINCENT DE PAUL CATHOLIC CHURCH

134 DAVENPORT JAIL

Built in 1914, this tiny two-cell town jail was only seldom used in its history. Once it held two young boys overnight after they stole a horse and took it for a joyride. Their incarceration was meant to teach them a lesson. More often, it was used as a place where local drunks could sleep it off. Why build a jail in this small town? Well, on the rare occasion one was needed, the 12-mile drive on the rough dirt road to Santa Cruz was too difficult and, at times, impossible. It was abandoned as a jail in 1936 after a new jail was built in Santa Cruz. Now owned and administered by the Museum of Art and History in Santa Cruz, the jail is open to the public for occasional tours. Contact the museum for details. Inside you'll find exhibits about the history of Davenport and the North Coast region.

■ **The Davenport Jail is on Center Street just off Highway 1, Davenport.**

THE TWO-CELL JAIL IS BUILT ENTIRELY OF POURED CONCRETE.

135 SWANTON PACIFIC RAILROAD

On the north coast of Santa Cruz, above Davenport, is the beautiful 3,200-acre Swanton Pacific Ranch. Bequeathed to California Polytechnic University by alumnus Al Smith in 1993, this property of redwood forest, cattle land and apple orchards is used by the Cal Poly College of Agriculture for instructional programs in forestry and agriculture. It is also the home of the Swanton Pacific Railroad (SPRR), with three miniature live-steam locomotives that are scaled to one-third standard size. They were originally built for the 1915 Panama-Pacific International Exposition and later purchased by Smith. In 1979, Smith began laying rails along Scott Creek to create a miniature railway. Since his death in 1993, the SPRR has been expanded and run by the Swanton Pacific Railroad Society. They have added a small-scale depot, a steel trestle over the creek and authentic signage. If you are lucky enough to get a chance to ride the train, you will travel in mostly open-air cars and meander through forest and meadow. You can also tour the property and see a diesel engine, a crane car, the roundhouse and turntable, the machine shop and an exhibit of Swanton historical memorabilia. Unfortunately, getting a chance to ride the trains usually only comes about twice a year during their annual Cal Poly Day in the fall and Al Smith Day in the spring. (Both events sell out quickly so you may want to become an SPRR member to get onto their list.) However, the public can walk around the property and see the tracks and equipment at other times, especially during their volunteer workdays that occur year-round on the second weekend of each month. For more information go to http://sprr.calpoly.edu.

■ **Swanton Pacific Railroad is located at 299 Swanton Road, Davenport.**

1914 PACIFIC LOCOMOTIVE

Photo courtesy Stephan Bianchi

THE GRIZZLY BEAR AT RANCHO DEL OSO NATURE CENTER

Did you know that the California grizzly bear once freely roamed Santa Cruz County? Prior to the arrival of the Spanish explorers, an estimated 133,000 grizzly bears lived in California. But modern weapons, traps, poisons and loss of habitat decimated their numbers: By 1922, the California Grizzly was considered extinct. Rancho del Oso (Ranch of the Bear) Nature Center, near the base of Waddell Valley,

GRIZZLY BEAR AKA *URSUS HORRIBILIS*

has a fascinating display about the history of grizzly bears in Santa Cruz County, including a 1,000-pound male grizzly bear specimen. Although not a California Grizzly, this bear, killed in Yellowstone National Park in 1920, reminds us of a time, not that distant, when grizzlies made their home here. In 1875, William Waddell, out hunting along his namesake creek, was killed by a grizzly. This was the last grizzly bear fatality in Santa Cruz County and possibly the last in California. In addition to the grizzly exhibit, Rancho del Oso Nature Center has a series of interactive exhibits that display the cultural and natural history of Waddell Valley, including the story of native peoples in the valley, the Spanish exploration camps, and the farming and timber industry. Light-up displays explain the ecology of the marshlands and Waddell Creek. Taxidermy-mounted animals including a mountain lion, a diving pelican, a bobcat, a fox and a badger are also on display. The center is open to the public only on weekends between noon and 4 p.m. To find the center, turn right onto the entrance road just before you get to the bridge on the Santa Cruz side of Waddell Creek. Go one-quarter mile down the dirt road.

■ **Rancho del Oso Nature Center is off Highway 1 across from Waddell Beach, 17 miles north of Santa Cruz.**

137 BONNY DOON ECOLOGICAL RESERVE

To see a unique sandhills habitat while also experiencing a stunning example of how forest and chaparral begin to recover after a devastating fire, visit the 552-acre Bonny Doon Ecological Reserve. Formed from an ancient seabed, the sandy soil of the reserve is home to many endangered plant species including the rare Santa Cruz wallflower and Ben Lomond spineflower, which are found only in the Santa Cruz Sandhills. In 2008, the Martin Fire burned 80 percent of the reserve and exposed geologic features that were previously hidden by the forest. A network of unmarked trails leads you through the burned-out forest, and the open landscape affords good views of the sandstone outcroppings on the hillside above the forest floor. The outcroppings are formations of Zayante sandstone, known locally as Moon Rocks because they resemble a lunar landscape. The Moon Rocks area is closed to the public, however, and trespassing is strictly prohibited. Parking for the reserve is in a small parking area off Martin Road next to the volunteer fire station.

■ The Bonny Doon Ecological Reserve is located at 975 Martin Road, Bonny Doon.

THE RESERVE IS MANAGED BY THE CALIFORNIA DEPARTMENT OF FISH AND WILDLIFE.

138 LOST WEEKEND BAR

OWNED AT ONE TIME BY GARY DAHL,
INVENTOR OF THE PET ROCK

For a little touch of North Coast history, take a short trip off Highway 1 and travel up Bonny Doon Road. In 2011, the Santa Cruz Museum of Art and History awarded one of its coveted blue plaques to a landmark building in the center of Bonny Doon. This historic building was the former home of the Lost Weekend Bar and, for 60 years, the community center for the town. It opened as the Bonny Doon Cash Store operated by Luigi and Mary Iacopetti in the 1920s. In 1950 it was renamed The Lost Weekend after the 1945 Billy Wilder movie starring Ray Milland as a writer who goes on a 4-day drinking binge. Over the years the building evolved into a tavern with food, drink, pool tables and a licensed card room. Its reign as The Lost Weekend ended in 1983 when it became a wine tasting room, originally for Bonny Doon Vineyard and now for Beauregard Vineyards. While the interior has been remodeled and expanded, you can still see blue chalk marks from pool cues on the wooden beams.

■ This landmark building is located in Bonny Doon at 10 Pine Flat Road.

139 BONNY DOON FIRE STATION MURAL

The Bonny Doon/Cal Fire Station, at the intersection of Empire Grade Road and Felton Empire Road, is graced with Bonny Doon's first public art project. Honoring the efforts of local firefighters who protect the Bonny Doon community, artist and Bonny Doon native Shanna Kuempel created an intricate 4-by-6-foot mural out of colorful handmade ceramic tiles. Commissioned by the County of Santa Cruz, the mural depicts two firefighters in full protective gear, standing ready, next to a relief map of Bonny Doon. The detailed map shows named roads, creeks, schools and churches. Since the map shows the entire area from the mountains to the

DETAIL OF THE CERAMIC MURAL

ocean, including local streams, it also provides a good aerial perspective on the relative location of Bonny Doon along the North Coast. To fully enjoy the map and the ceramic artistry, you need to see it up close.

■ The fire station and mural are located about 8 miles north of the intersection of Bay and High Streets at 7276 Empire Grade Road.

EASTSIDE SANTA CRUZ

Santa Cruz's Eastside has wonderful sunny neighborhoods and a long history. It is generally considered to be the area east of the San Lorenzo River, including the neighborhoods of Seabright, Branciforte, Delavega and for the purposes of this book, Live Oak. Now mostly residential except along the major thoroughfares, the Eastside has great beaches, the small craft harbor, an 18-hole golf course and many small parks.

LIGHTHOUSE AT THE HARBOR

A short walk out to the end of the jetty at the Santa Cruz Small Craft Harbor will give you an up-close-and-personal look at the modern but classically styled Walton Lighthouse. Standing 42 feet tall at the opening to the harbor, this fully functional lighthouse was built to replace the original utilitarian structures with something more elegant and picturesque. Designed by Mark Mesiti-Miller and dedicated in 2002, the lighthouse weighs 350,000 pounds. In the winter, when waves wash over the jetty and crash against the lighthouse, you can understand why it was built with 4.5-foot-thick walls at the base to withstand a quarter-million pounds of wave energy. Within

the copper-roofed lantern room at the top of the lighthouse, a green light flashes every 4 seconds to welcome and warn boats and ships. The path along the jetty is flat, friendly and a popular place for walkers and joggers when the bay is calm. During stormy weather or when the surf is up, walking out to the lighthouse can become dangerous and should be avoided.

■ **The lighthouse can be reached from the west side of the harbor at the end of Atlantic Avenue in Santa Cruz.**

THE LIGHTHOUSE RISES 42 FEET ABOVE THE JETTY,
20 FEET HIGHER THAN THE TOWER IT REPLACED.

THE SANTA CRUZ SMALL CRAFT HARBOR

The Santa Cruz Small Craft Harbor (aka The Yacht Harbor) was built on the site of the former Woods Lagoon in 1963. The picturesque walk around the harbor from the Walton Lighthouse on the west side to the Crow's Nest restaurant on the east side is 1.9 miles and offers great views of the myriad of boats berthed there, including about 500 pleasure sailboats, 350 pleasure powerboats and 150 commercial fishing boats. You will also see paddleboarders, kayakers and maybe even sunbathing sea lions.

■ **The harbor is located in the Eastside of Santa Cruz between Seabright and Seventh Avenues, near the Murray Street Bridge.**

141 HARBOR SIGNPOSTS

A special treat can be had by stopping at one or more of the many yellow and blue harbor signposts that are spaced every 100 or so yards in strategic locations around the harbor. Below each signpost you will discover colorful displays with detailed descriptions of life at the harbor and in the Monterey Bay. To understand more about sailing, read Evolution of Sailing Vessels, Physics of Sailing or History of the Marine Compass. To learn more about wildlife, check out Birds of the Santa Cruz Small Craft Harbor, Some Marine Mammals of Monterey Bay, and Whales of Monterey Bay and the Monterey Bay Sanctuary. You can also learn about the tides, commercial fishing, harbor dredging, trees around the harbor, and much more.

LOOK FOR THE YELLOW AND BLUE SIGNPOSTS.

142 GIANT JACKS OF THE JETTY

If you have made it out onto the harbor jetty near the lighthouse, you may have been intrigued by the giant "jacks" that line the outer surface of the west jetty. Called tetrapods because of their four legs, they are made out of reinforced concrete and weigh 25 tons each. Their shape allows them to easily interlock while dissipating the force of incoming waves. Nine hundred of them were manufactured locally near 17th Avenue and Brommer Street, transported individually to the harbor, and put into place by a crane. Look carefully to see if you can find the one with the heart-shaped "love" mosaic attached to its side.

GIANT JACKS PROTECT THE HARBOR.

143 MILE BUOY

You've probably never seen it, but if you live anywhere near the coastline in Santa Cruz, you've probably heard it. One mile directly south of the harbor entrance, a 26-foot-high lighted whistle buoy floats on the waves. On quiet evenings its low-pitched moan, powered by wave action, can be heard calling sailors and neighbors alike. Attached to its 12,700-pound anchor by a 260-foot mooring chain, the buoy flashes a white light every 5 seconds and serves as a reference point for vessels without navigation equipment. Stand on the cliffs near the harbor with a good pair of binoculars and see if you can spot this elusive creature.

Photo courtesy Christian Riblet

LISTEN FOR A LOW-PITCHED MOAN LATE AT NIGHT.

144 HUMAN SUNDIAL

Here is your chance to be a gnomon, the part of a sundial that sticks up and casts a shadow to tell you the time. On the beach side of the shops next to the Crow's Nest at the Santa Cruz Small Craft Harbor, you will find an excellent example of a human

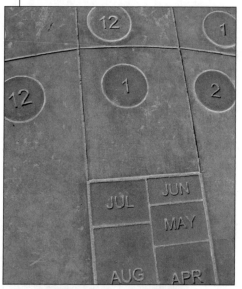

NO WATCH? NO PROBLEM. JUST STAND AND TELL THE TIME WITH YOUR SHADOW.

sundial. Colored markers in the cement are arrayed in a semicircular pattern around a boxed set of 12 rectangles that indicate the months of the year. Stand on the square representing the current month and look down to follow your shadow. There are two rings of circular hour markers; the outer ring is for Standard Time, the inner ring is for Daylight Savings Time. Where your shadow falls indicates the time. To get an exact reading, it helps to be very skinny or have a pointy head. This colorful sundial, designed by Leslie Stone Associates (LSA), is easy to use and surprisingly accurate. And if it is an overcast day, you can always just while away the time at one of the nearby restaurants and enjoy the ocean view.

SANTA CRUZ MUSEUM OF NATURAL HISTORY

Housed in the historical former Seabright Branch Library building, the more than 100-year-old Santa Cruz Museum of Natural History provides a fascinating look at thousands of years of Santa Cruz history. Sometimes called "the whale museum" by locals because of the life-sized whale sculpture that sits outside, the museum's permanent exhibits include a history of the native peoples of Santa Cruz, local geology and fossils (including the skull of a mastodon), extensive dioramas of local wildlife, a tidal touch pool, an active beehive and many hands-on displays. Additional featured exhibits throughout the year make every visit a new experience.

■ **The Santa Cruz Museum of Natural History is located at 1305 East Cliff Drive.**

145 OHLONE INDIAN EXHIBIT

THE MURAL SHOWS A TYPICAL OHLONE VILLAGE.

Want to imagine what it was like to live in Santa Cruz hundreds of years ago before the arrival of Europeans? The museum's "Native Peoples of Santa Cruz" exhibit room has a huge 9-by-17-foot wall mural by local artist Ann Thiermann. It depicts a typical Ohlone village, with scenes of people cooking, grinding acorns, weaving, hunting and gathering. Dome-shaped houses are made of woven mats of tule rushes (common in California wetlands) placed over bent willow poles. Women are wearing traditional skirts of tule or shredded bark fronts with tanned deerskin backs. Men and children are wearing nothing, as they did for most of the year. The room also holds examples of Ohlone baskets, hunting and fishing tools, shell necklaces, and mortars and pestles for preparing acorns to make mush and bread.

146 THE LIVE HONEYBEE COLONY

To get a safe, up-close-and-personal look at the goings-on in a typical honeybee colony, check out the wood and glass enclosed hive on display at the back of the museum. Put your face near the glass and see the queen bee's nest, hundreds of female worker bees and the occasional drone. During the day you will see a constant flow of bees leaving and entering the hive through a clear tube that exits the building near the back door.

SEE THE COMINGS AND GOINGS OF BEES.

147 THE MOUNTAIN LION GUARDING THE BACK ROOM

MALE MOUNTAIN LIONS WEIGH 130 TO 150 POUNDS AND CAN BE 8 FEET LONG.

If you hike in the Santa Cruz Mountains, you will hear or read warnings about mountain lions. Perhaps you have even been one of the few who have caught sight of this elusive creature. But if not, go to the back room of the Santa Cruz Museum of Natural History and you will see—looming over you—a male mountain lion that was shot and killed in the foothills near Carmel in December, 1981. You can't help but be impressed by the size and strength of this old male as he watches you from his perch above. Normally shy and solitary, mountain lions usually avoid people and attacks on humans are extremely uncommon. (According to the California Department of Fish and Wildlife, between 1890 and 2007 there were only 16 verified attacks and six fatalities from mountain lions in California.) The museum also has other taxidermy specimens including a skunk, bobcat, fox and hawks.

148 THE TAPERTAIL RIBBONFISH

In 1938, Italian fisherman August "Gus" Canepa caught a strange fish off the Santa Cruz Municipal Wharf. Thin as a pancake, but over 6-feet-3-inches long with a bright red fin stretching from head to tail, the tapertail ribbonfish was put on ice and displayed at the Santa Cruz City Museum where it became a local sensation.

Since ribbonfish normally live at great depths in the ocean, it was highly unusual to find such a beautifully intact specimen. It was so unusual, in fact, the Smithsonian Institute in Washington, D.C., heard about it and wanted it for their collection. The museum agreed to give it to them in exchange for a cast of the prize fish. Stop by the Santa Cruz Museum of Natural History to see the cast of this magnificent specimen.

A MOST UNUSUAL FISH

149 GRAY WHALE SCULPTURE

She is a life-sized female gray whale, 38 feet long. Unlike most gray whales, who every year make the 12,500-mile round trip along the coast between Alaska and the Baja Peninsula, this slate-gray lady with painted barnacles lounges year-round in front of the Santa Cruz Museum of Natural History. She was created in 1982 by sculptor Larry Foster, a world renowned whale artist, and fabricator Al Hipkins. This iconic Seabright sculpture has been climbed and played on by thousands of neighborhood kids (and some parents) ever since. In 2009, she was repainted and filled with concrete and now

TWENTY THOUSAND GRAY WHALES MIGRATE PAST SANTA CRUZ EVERY YEAR, BUT THIS ONE STAYS HERE.

weighs 36 tons, about the same weight as a real gray whale. She is your one chance to ride on the back of a whale without getting wet.

■ **The Santa Cruz Museum of Natural History is located at 1305 East Cliff Drive.**

150 OCEAN VIEW PARK SLIDES

Santa Cruz has lots of neighborhood parks and most of them have slides. But none can compete with the 40-foot-long metal slides at Ocean View Park. Built on a hillside, the slides are only inches above the ground, so there is no danger of a big fall. The two side-by-side slides are perfect for racing down with friends or family. People often bring along waxed paper to speed up the run, but be careful, the slides

THESE SLIDES ARE AS FUN AND FAST AS THEY LOOK.

can get really fast. There is one bump near the bottom and then a short glide where you either stop or get plopped into an area of sand and dirt. Ocean View Park also has a large play structure with conventional curving plastic slides and swings, and a large grassy play area for kids and dogs. But the real joy is racing down those metal slides.

■ **Ocean View Park is located at 102 Ocean View Avenue.**

151 OCEAN VIEW AVENUE HISTORIC HOMES

A one-third-mile stroll down Ocean View Avenue, beginning at Broadway and ending at Ocean View Park, will take you past some of the grandest homes in Santa Cruz and is a study of how the city's elite lived in the late 19th century. These magnificent homes showcase a variety of architectural styles including Eastlake, Stick-Eastlake, Queen Anne and Colonial Revival. Many of the homes still have their original spacious gardens with mature magnolias, palms and other large trees. Ocean View Avenue runs along a terrace above the San Lorenzo River and was opened to development in 1871. Start your walk at the elaborate Stick-Eastlake house, at 412 Ocean View Avenue, built in 1880 and decorated with Swiss Chalet trim. Farther down the street, at 317 Ocean View Avenue, is a simple home designed by LeBaron Olive and built in 1891. It was originally a twin to the Eastlake-style mansion at 250 Ocean View Avenue that still has its original carriage house. Notice the interesting corner tower with its zigzag cornice line. The house at 245 Ocean View Avenue was built circa 1877 in the Italianate style and in the 1880s, a Stick-Eastlake-style front was added. These are only a few of the many elaborate homes here. As you walk down the avenue, see if you can find the curbside horse post, a remnant of another time when horses were the dominant form of transportation.

■ **Ocean View Avenue is located off Broadway, east of Ocean Street, in Santa Cruz.**

EASTLAKE-STYLE MANSION AT 250 OCEAN VIEW AVENUE

152 KEN WORMHOUDT SKATE PARK

Interested in seeing skateboarders in action? In February 2007, Santa Cruz, already home to what is widely believed to be the world's first public skate park (Derby Park on the Westside off Woodland Way), opened the new state-of-the-art Ken

Wormhoudt Skate Park. Designed by Wormhoudt's son Zach, this 15,000-square-foot park has two deep bowls, a 17-foot full pipe, a practice bowl, a street course with steps, hubba ledges, wall rides and metal rails. It is used by young skaters and seasoned pros. The beautifully designed park incorporates public art by artists Judi Oyama and Jimbo Phillips (full pipe wave art) and Dave Gardner (bowl

THE 17-FOOT-TALL FULL PIPE MIMICS AN OCEAN WAVE.

designs). You can watch the skaters from bleachers next to the park or head up to the San Lorenzo River levee path above the park for an even better view. It is located just a few blocks from the Boardwalk and Downtown Santa Cruz.

■ **Ken Wormhoudt Skate Park is located at 225 San Lorenzo Boulevard at Riverside Avenue, Santa Cruz.**

153 SANTA CRUZ ART LEAGUE

There is always something new and different happening at this venerable art gallery on the Santa Cruz Eastside. Since 1919, the Santa Cruz Art League has provided local

SANTA CRUZ ART LEAGUE, SINCE 1919

and regional artists of all types with a place to exhibit their work, take workshops, teach others and share ideas. The Art League has been housed in their current location on Broadway for more than 50 years and their exhibit hall, theater and gift shop have seen the works of generations of artists. The Art League hosts 12 to 14 exhibits every year including the annual spring High School Show that features the best student artists from around the county; the annual Statewide Exhibition that has been held in Santa Cruz for over 80 years; and the not-to-be-missed Open Studios Preview every fall. The Art League also sells paintings, postcards, ceramics, jewelry and glassware by local artists.

■ **The Santa Cruz Art League is located at 526 Broadway, Santa Cruz.**

STAR OF THE SEA WINDOWS

One of the great artistic treasures of Santa Cruz is a series of carved-glass window panels at Our Lady Star of the Sea Catholic Church. Artist Heather Robyn Matthews was commissioned to design and carve twelve 3-by-12-foot glass panels depicting water scenes from the Bible. "The Ark" shows Noah's boat at rest after the great flood. "Moses in the Reeds" shows baby Moses' basket among the bulrushes. "Parting of the Red Sea" is a powerful two-panel depiction of huge waves being held back to help the Israelites who were fleeing Egypt. Throughout the series, Matthews incorporates local flowers, birds and animals into the imagery and, if you look carefully, you can see a California poppy, a brown pelican, redwood tree branches, a monarch butterfly and other local flora and fauna. When Matthews designed "Miraculous Catch of Fish," she used cork floats on the fishing nets in honor of the early Sicilians in Santa Cruz (she also depicted local salmon, rock cod and jellyfish). Her intricate carvings on three-eighths-inch bronze glass create a layered, multidimensional effect and on sunny days, the works are

Photo courtesy Tim Matthews for Heather Robyn Matthews/Heather Glass

"WATER FROM THE ROCK"

especially stunning. The simplicity of the 1948 Spanish Colonial Revival church complements the beauty of these translucent windows. The works can be seen before or after Mass, or at other times when the church is open.

■ **Our Lady Star of the Sea Catholic Church is located at 515 Frederick Street, Santa Cruz.**

THIS CLOSE-UP OF A PEREGRINE SHOWS THE EXQUISITE LEVEL OF DETAIL IN THE WINDOWS.

Photo courtesy Tim Matthews

THE BRIDGE MOSAICS

The bridges over the San Lorenzo River that connect the Eastside of Santa Cruz to the Downtown are not just essential transportation corridors; they also now showcase colorful glass mosaics that are both beautiful and educational. In 2011, Mission Hill students, under the direction of artist Kathleen Crocetti, created and placed 53 mosaics on the lampposts of the Water Street Bridge. On both sides of the bridge you will see mosaics of plants and animals of the San Lorenzo River watershed including many endangered species. Monarch butterflies, steelhead salmon, pelicans, sea otters, yellow-billed cuckoos, lupin, and California poppies are all on display. In 2012, Crocetti and her students took on another project and decorated the lampposts of the Soquel Avenue Bridge with images of agricultural products of Santa Cruz County. The 92 different mosaics include vegetables (turnips, squash, onions), fruit (olallieberry, pear, apples), herbs (fennel, bay leaf, sage), as well as chickens, cattle and sheep. Finally, in 2013, it was Laurel Street Bridge's turn to get a mosaic makeover. The bridge's 26 lampposts are decorated with 86 different scenes of Pacific Ocean marine life, including jellyfish, seahorses, dolphins, sharks, whales, shorebirds, and lots of tide pool creatures. Walking the bridges to get a close-up view helps you appreciate not only the creative artwork of these young people, but also the abundance of plant, animal and marine life that enriches Santa Cruz County.

■ **The mosaics are located on both sides of the Water Street, Soquel Avenue and Laurel Street Bridges in Santa Cruz.**

"GREAT HORNED OWL" BY ASA SCHAEFFER
AND TYLER SAMUELSON

"AVOCADO" BY ASPEN SCHWIND AND
ISABEL WHITTAKER-WALKER

3,000-TILE MURAL

MURAL DETAIL

Hidden at the back of the parking lot behind the Eastside fire station is a massive community-created mural. Three thousand, two hundred and twenty-four glass-on-ceramic tiles were individually designed by students and teachers from 11 Santa Cruz schools. The tiles were placed together to generate a huge mosaic, approximately 6 feet high and 100 feet long; then blue, black, red and white-colored grout was used to create a swirling abstract pattern that runs the length of the mural. The colorful geometric design is adapted from the work of French artist Sonia Delaunay. To really appreciate the mural, you need to get up close and admire the playful and whimsical hand-crafted tiles—each one different. Led by artist and teacher Kathleen Crocetti, the project is part of a series of community-created murals throughout the county.

■ **The mural is located at the back of the parking lot at 1111 Soquel Avenue, Santa Cruz.**

SIX HUNDRED POUNDS OF GLASS WENT INTO CREATING THIS MASSIVE MURAL.

157 THE MYSTERY SPOT

Yes, it is hokey, and you can find gravity defying "mystery spots" in other tourist locations, but the Mystery Spot in Santa Cruz has been around since 1940 and is world famous. It will challenge your senses and—even though you know you are

TAKE HOME ONE OF THEIR UBIQUITOUS
BUMPER STICKERS.

not seeing what you think you are seeing—you cannot help but be intrigued and amused. Located in a redwood forest, the Mystery Spot, purported to be 150 feet in diameter, is a place where "it appears as though every law of gravitation has gone haywire." When you visit, you will be taken on a 45-minute guided tour where you will personally see and feel the effects of the mystery (as well as hear many corny jokes). Billiard balls will appear to roll uphill, your shorter friend will suddenly seem taller than you, and you can lean at a 70-degree angle without falling over. It is inexpensive and worth checking out at least once.

■ **Located off Branciforte Drive a short distance beyond DeLaveaga Park at 465 Mystery Spot Road, Santa Cruz.**

158 GREAT BLUE HERON WALKWAY

Take a look at these giant colorful birds. On a small grassy knoll in Jose Avenue Park in Live Oak stand two 6-foot-tall blue herons. Created by artists Sandra Whiting and Barbara Abbott, these steel-and-cement sculptures are covered with colorful mosaic pieces donated by members of the neighborhood. Take a closer look and you will see teacups and other broken pottery and glass, buttons, a spoon, a key, Elvis memorabilia, bottle caps and porcelain animal figurines. This small park has basketball courts, a skateboard bowl, a children's playground, picnic areas and, scattered throughout the park, more than 40 great blue heron footprints embedded in the concrete pathways. See how many you can find.

■ **Enter Jose Avenue Park from Jose Avenue off Capitola Road or from Eddy Lane off Seventh Avenue, Santa Cruz.**

THIS BLUE HERON IS PART OF THE SANTA
CRUZ COUNTY PUBLIC ART PROGRAM.

159 SCHWAN LAKE PARK

Hidden in the Eastside of Santa Cruz, behind the Simpkins Family Swim Center, is a small park with hiking trails, old oaks and eucalyptus trees, and wonderful views of Schwan Lake (also known as Schwan Lagoon). Schwan Lake is one of two lakes that

THIS PARK IS A LITTLE HARD TO FIND, BUT IT IS A HIDDEN GEM AND WORTH A VISIT.

gave this area the name Twin Lakes. The other was Woods Lagoon, which was dredged in 1961 and converted into the Santa Cruz Small Craft Harbor. Schwan Lake Park is home to ducks, geese and seabirds. The 1.1-mile trail through the park is made up of two loops shaped like a backward *B*. The furthest loop affords great views of the lake and beyond to Twin Lakes State Beach and the bay. This quiet and uncrowded park is a great place for a quick picnic or a romantic walk.

The trailhead is at the back of the Simpkins Center parking lot, near a small sign and information panel. The beginning of the trail parallels the railroad tracks.

■ **Schwan Lake Park is located behind the Simpkins Family Swim Center at 979 17th Avenue, Santa Cruz.**

160 HISTORIC SCHOOL BELL

To see a big and beautiful cast-iron bell from the turn of the last century, visit the display in front of the current Live Oak Elementary School. You will find the bell that used to ring from the tower of the original 1914 one-room Live Oak School. In 2009,

after having sat outside next to a woodpile for decades, the bell was donated back to the school by longtime resident David Branum. The rust-encrusted bell was cleaned, painted and restored with new parts. The black iron bell now hangs in a replica wood and brick cupola on the school grounds, along with a bronze plaque showing an illustration of the 1914 schoolhouse. The bell is a great reminder for students and local residents of Live Oak's historic past.

■ **The Live Oak School Bell is located at 1916 Capitola Road, Santa Cruz.**

AFTER 50 YEARS, THE BELL IS BACK WHERE IT BELONGS.

MID-COUNTY: CAPITOLA, SOQUEL, APTOS, RIO DEL MAR

The Mid-County region includes the quaint towns of Capitola, Soquel, Aptos and Rio del Mar. There are many beaches, stunning ocean views and dense redwood forests here, as well as local museums, historic buildings and Cabrillo College.

161 CAPITOLA WHARF

The 855-foot wooden Capitola Wharf is a place for fishing, a short stroll out over the water, and fabulous views of Capitola Village and the mountains beyond. For many, the fishing is the real draw and, along with the crash of the waves and the screech of the gulls, you'll hear talk of what type of bait works best and the big one that got away. Some anglers fish from the wharf or you can rent a boat. There is also a bait shop. You can

THE PEDESTRIAN-FRIENDLY CAPITOLA WHARF

catch various types of fish here and the species you find depends upon where you fish. Close to the sandy beach, you will find barred and calico surfperch, and farther out (in deeper water) there are white croaker, smaller species of perch, flounder, sole, sand dabs and halibut. At the far end of the wharf there are striped bass and even several varieties of shark. Take your family or friends and try your luck fishing on a sunny afternoon, or just take a stroll out to the end of the wharf and enjoy the view.

■ **The Capitola Wharf is located at Cliff Drive and Wharf Road, Capitola.**

THE CAPITOLA WHARF WAS FIRST COMPLETED IN 1857.

162 CAPITOLA HISTORICAL MUSEUM

The Capitola Historical Museum is a tiny 1920s farm cottage in downtown Capitola. Packed with a collection of photographs and artifacts from Capitola's past, it is the perfect place to visit if you are interested in local history. The museum hosts changing exhibits on seasonal and topical themes. Past exhibits have included "Capitola in the 1950s," "History of Women Surfing," "A Century of Swimwear," and "A History of the Arts in Capitola." Museum volunteers are able to answer many questions you might have about Capitola's history.

■ **The Capitola Historical Museum and Beach Cottage are at 410 Capitola Avenue, Capitola.**

THE CAPITOLA HISTORICAL MUSEUM IS ON THE LEFT, THE BEACH COTTAGE ON THE RIGHT.

163 BEACH COTTAGE

The one-room beach cottage on display at the Capitola Historical Museum is tiny, but in the early part of the last century, $1-a-day cottages like this were home to many seaside tourists visiting the beaches of Capitola and Santa Cruz. Vacationers would stay on the coast for a month or more during summer to get away from California's hotter regions. Since the cottages were not plumbed, camp bathhouses like the one on display next to the cottage were used for bathing. The accommodations were simple but cozy. The cottage at the museum was built in 1907 and was used in Santa Cruz Beach Boardwalk's Cottage City for more than 30 years. Sold in 1941 to help make way for a new parking lot, the cottage was moved from Santa Cruz to Capitola where it was used for 60 years in an Oak Avenue backyard. About to be demolished in 2004, the City of Capitola relocated it next to the museum and restored it in 2007 as an example of what beach living was like. Peek in the windows and you will see how such a cottage might have been furnished in those early days of seaside tourism.

164 TIKI

At the end of the Capitola Esplanade, squatting beside a short palm tree is a 3-foot tiki carving with a toothy grimace and eyes squinting out toward the bay. A local surfing group installed the first tiki here in 2008 without permission, creating a community controversy. After city officials ordered the carving removed, tiki supporters rallied to successfully bring it back. But it didn't stay for long—within months it was stolen. "It's bad karma," the Capitola police chief was quoted as saying. Sadly, the original tiki was never recovered. Local Capitola carver Wilhelm Zilliacus came to the rescue and donated one of his tikis to the city. It was dedicated during Capitola's 60th birthday celebration in 2009. The Capitola Art & Cultural Commission said that the new tiki had "good juju." Stroll down to Esplanade Park to see the tiki yourself. If you're tempted to run off with it, think again. To prevent theft, the statue was installed using 14 sacks of cement and a heavy steel rod. For good measure, a GPS chip was embedded inside. This tiki is staying right where it is.

■ You'll find the tiki in Esplanade Park, Capitola.

THE TIKI IN ESPLANADE PARK

165 CAPITOLA TILE SEAWALL

More than 1,200 wildly colorful tiles decorate the seawall along the Capitola Esplanade, all part of an ambitious 2008 community project to beautify the otherwise uninteresting cement wall. The theme, developed by the Capitola Art & Cultural Commission, is "Capitola Memories—Sand, Sun and Sea." Petroglyph, a local ceramics studio, provided instruction, glazes and firing. Families, children and visitors to Capitola decorated the tiles with images of their Capitola Beach memories. You can see paintings of fish only a child can imagine, beach scenes, views of Capitola landmarks, sunsets and much more.

BEACH MEMORIES ALONG THE TILE SEA WALL

■ The tile seawall is located along the Capitola Esplanade.

166 VENETIAN COURT

Situated almost directly on Capitola Beach, you can't miss the Venetian Court, the first seaside condominium complex in California. Built in 1924, the complex is a fantastical Mediterranean design reminiscent of buildings in Venice, Italy. Tiny row-

VENETIAN COURT ON CAPITOLA BEACH

house dwellings separated by narrow alleys face the beach. The houses all have a swirling waterlike stucco finish and are decorated with imaginary sea creatures, painted tiles or built-in urns. Many houses are brightly colored in pastels of Pepto-Bismol pink, pistachio green or aqua blue. The complex is a mixture of privately owned units and others rented out by the Capitola Venetian Hotel. The Venetian Court is listed on the National Register of Historic Places.

■ **The Venetian Court condominiums are located at 1500 Wharf Road, Capitola.**

167 DEASY PARK BLUFF TRAIL

Capitola has many beautiful views. One of the best is the view from the bluffs on the west side of town. Perhaps the best time to see this panorama of the Capitola Wharf, Capitola Village, Depot Hill, and the beaches beyond is at sunset as the waning light illuminates the village. You can take a short walk along the narrow dirt trail that

travels above the railroad tracks at the top of the bluff behind the homes on Prospect Avenue. Start your walk by enjoying the view from one of the benches in Deasy Park. Then follow the trail to the staircase and down to Wharf Road. From there it is a very short walk to the Stockton Avenue Bridge and into Capitola Village.

■ **Access the trail at Deasy Park, near Prospect and 49th Avenues, above Cliff Drive in Capitola.**

WALKING TRAIL TOWARD WHARF ROAD

168 CAPITOLA TRESTLE

The Capitola Trestle that spans Soquel Creek is one of Capitola Village's most prominent landmarks. The trestle was first built in 1874 for the Santa Cruz–Watsonville Railroad, the same year Camp Capitola was founded by entrepreneur

TRESTLE FROM THE STOCKTON AVENUE BRIDGE

Frederick Hihn. The railroad was part of Hihn's plan to bring tourists to his new resort on the Monterey Bay. The trestle was reconstructed for broad-gauge use in 1884 and has undergone a series of alterations since that time. Until recently, trains rumbled across the trestle several times each week. Some daring pedestrians use the trestle as a shortcut over the creek. During the annual Capitola Begonia Festival on Labor Day weekend, begonia-decorated floats pass under the trestle while crowds cheer from above. Your best view of the trestle is from the Stockton Avenue Bridge at the mouth of Soquel Creek.

■ **The Capitola Trestle is located in Capitola Village.**

169 THE HILLAVATOR

Shadowbrook Restaurant offers a unique way to get to its front door: via an inclined elevator the restaurant calls a "hillavator." Your ride begins at street level and the car slowly descends the angled 118-foot track. You glide down through the restaurant's lush gardens, past palm trees, ferns and a beautiful waterfall, to be finally delivered at the restaurant entrance and bar. The whole trip takes about a minute. Up to six passengers can squeeze into the wood-paneled car, which is also wheelchair accessible. But if you prefer to go at your own pace and enjoy the gardens close-up, you can follow the steep footpath down. The choice is yours.

■ **Shadowbrook Restaurant is located at 1750 Wharf Road, Capitola.**

THE HILLAVATOR TAKES YOU DOWN TO SHADOWBROOK RESTAURANT.

170 RISPIN MANSION

The historic Rispin Mansion is hidden in a cluster of trees above Soquel Creek in Capitola. Wealthy San Franciscan, Henry Allen Rispin, built the solid-cement, 22-room mansion in 1921. Rispin had purchased the resort of Capitola from the heir of its first owner, Frederick Hihn, and had grand plans to further develop the area—but by 1928, Rispin had lost his fortune and his showcase home. The mansion had several subsequent owners including the Catholic Church, which used the building as a convent until 1957. Officially vacant since then, the building was the target of destructive vandalism and became an eyesore. The City of Capitola bought the property in 1985 and considered various proposals for its use, including making the mansion into an upscale hotel. Those plans ended after a 2009 fire caused significant damage. In 2011, after rejecting proposals to demolish the structure, the City of Capitola repaired the Spanish-style building and prepared it to be the centerpiece of a planned community park. The mansion looks like an old California Mission surrounded by mature trees. As you walk along the property, imagine how it looked in the past, and what it could become in the future.

■ **The Rispin Mansion is located at 2200 Wharf Road, Capitola, across the street from the Capitola Public Library.**

HOPEFULLY, THIS 7,000-SQUARE-FOOT MANSION WILL ONE DAY BE RESTORED.

171 AVERON-LODGE HOUSE

Hidden behind Capitola Mansion Apartments is the oldest structure in Capitola, the Averon-Lodge House. This was the final residence of Martina Castro, granddaughter of Joaquin Isidro Castro who made the historic trek from Sonora, Mexico, to the San Francisco Bay with the Anza Expedition in 1776. The house stands on what was the last tiny sliver of Martina Castro's once vast land holdings, 34,000-acres of Mexican land grants, which extended from Monterey Bay to the base of Loma Prieta and included much of today's Capitola and Soquel. Martina died in the house in 1890. Her daughters, who inherited the property, gradually sold pieces of the land in order to pay ever-increasing property taxes; and in 1972, Martina's remaining heirs were forced to sell the mansard-roofed house to developers. Preservationists fought to save the home as an important piece of local history. There were dreams of making it a museum. Instead, the once open land was filled with apartments and the house was converted to offices.

■ **Walk behind the Capitola Mansion Apartments to view this important piece of Capitola history at 919 Capitola Avenue, Capitola.**

THE AVERON-LODGE HOUSE IS THE OLDEST HOUSE IN CAPITOLA.

CAPITOLA RIVERVIEW WALK

Along Soquel Creek in Capitola is a charming footpath that winds alongside the creek, past small historic cottages, bungalows, and tiny gardens that go right down to the water's edge. Some of the cottages are private homes and others are vacation rentals but all are wonderfully whimsical with close-up views of creeklife as it glides lazily by. As you walk the path, you will pass under the Capitola Trestle, one of the few of its kind remaining in California. You will also see the Windmill House, an unusual structure built in 1926 that resembles the base of a windmill. Then you will encounter Old Riverview Court, a tiny Spanish-style courtyard apartment complex built in 1921. The pathway, which is about the length of a football field, passes through private waterfront gardens, many of which are furnished with tables and chairs perched on tiny patios and neatly landscaped and maintained decks.

■ **The path starts on the east side of Stockton Avenue Bridge in the Old Riverview Historic District in Capitola.**

THIS FOOTPATH FOLLOWS SOQUEL CREEK PAST TINY GARDENS AND HISTORIC COTTAGES.

173 DEPOT HILL CLIFF TRAIL

THE VIEW FROM DEPOT HILL

For a panoramic view of Monterey Bay from up high, take the walking trail along the cliffs above the bay on Depot Hill in Capitola. This irregular path is part dirt and part pavement, wide in some places and narrow in others where giant chunks of hillside have eroded into the bay, destroying much of what was once Grand Avenue. On a clear day, you can see as far as Monterey. You will join joggers and walkers, and people just leaning against the fence and taking it all in. You will see waves forming in the distance, rolling one after another toward shore, and surfers as they choose their waves and ride to the beach. The cliff is so high you will find yourself eye-level with gulls and pelicans gliding along the arc of the coastline.

■ **The walkway extends from Cliff Avenue to Hollister Avenue.**

174 DEPOT HILL STAIRCASES

There are two staircases that climb from Capitola Village up to Cliff Avenue on Depot Hill. The Hihn Park Staircase starts at Monterey Avenue and travels via Porter Path to Hihn Park, a tiny perch on Cliff Avenue that is decorated with old anchors, ropes and chains. It is a charming resting place created and maintained by neighbors. You can also climb the 86 steps from El Camino Medio Street. It's a steep staircase, but the broad views of Capitola and the Monterey Bay are worth the trip.

■ **Both staircases take you from Capitola Village to the top of Depot Hill.**

AN 86-STEP CLIMB CONNECTS EL CAMINO MEDIO STREET TO CLIFF AVENUE.

175 SURFERS AT PLEASURE POINT

If you want to watch surfers in action, one of the most scenic spots in the county is the 1-mile-round-trip path along East Cliff Drive between 41st Avenue and Pleasure Point. Along this stretch of coastline is a series of surf breaks with names such as The Hook, The Drain Pipe, "once in a whiles," The Dirt Farm, Suicides and Sewer Peak. Always dozens, and sometimes hundreds, of surfers can be seen in the water, riding or getting ready to ride the waves. A good viewing area is above The Hook, at the end of 41st Avenue across from the parking lot and restrooms. The Hook often has waves that break inside close to the rocks, providing close-ups of surfers from the edge of the cliff. More surfing can be seen at the small cliffside park near the end of 37th Avenue. This "dirt farm," popular with dog owners, has benches with great views. As you walk the path along the cliffs you will also see some interesting oceanfront homes, including a few perched directly on the cliffs above the water. Together with Steamer Lane off West Cliff Drive in Santa Cruz, Pleasure Point is one

of the best-known surfing locations on the West Coast. Bring your camera and binoculars and enjoy watching both the magnificent waves and the wetsuit-clad men and women who surf them.

■ **Pleasure Point is on East Cliff Drive between 32nd and 41st Avenues, Santa Cruz.**

WATCH SOME OF THE WORLD'S GREATEST SURFERS.

176 THE CEMENT SHIP

From the ocean bluffs of Capitola, Aptos or Rio del Mar, you can get a magnificent view of the remains of the S.S. (steamship) *Palo Alto*, which juts out from Seacliff State Beach. The concrete S.S. *Palo Alto* is known as the Cement Ship. She was one of three concrete ships built at the end of World War I by the San Francisco Shipbuilding Company. Designed as an oil tanker, the 425-foot ship never saw service and sat in San Francisco Bay until 1929, when she was purchased by the Seacliff Amusement Company and towed to what is now Seacliff State Beach. The *Palo Alto* was grounded in shallow water off the beach and connected to the shore by a 600-foot-long pier. She was then converted into an "amusement ship" with a café, dance hall (Rain-Bow Ball Room), swimming pool and carnival-like attractions. Two years later, in the midst of the Great Depression, the Seacliff Amusement Company went bankrupt. The ship was severely damaged in a winter storm and converted into a fishing pier. Over the years, additional storm damage made the ship increasingly unsafe and in 2000, the ship was permanently closed. You can still go out onto the wooden pier for a close-up look at the pelicans, cormorants, and other seabirds who have taken over this storied vessel. Be sure to stop by the Seacliff State Beach visitor center to see early photographs, a scale model of the original S.S. *Palo Alto* and a short video that gives an entertaining tour of the ship before she was closed to the public.

■ **The Cement Ship is located at Seacliff State Beach via the State Park Drive exit off Highway 1 in Aptos.**

THE CEMENT SHIP IS NOW HOME TO SEABIRDS AND MARINE LIFE.

NEW BRIGHTON STATE BEACH

New Brighton State Beach is a 93-acre park with a half-mile-long beach backed by a bluff that contains a forested campground, picnic areas and wonderful ocean views. The site of a Chinese fishing village in the 1870s and 1880s, the beach area near the cliffs is sometimes called China Cove and is a common surf-fishing spot. A state beach since 1933, New Brighton is one of the most popular beaches in California.

■ The entrance to New Brighton State Beach is located in Capitola on the frontage road just south of the Park Avenue exit on Highway 1.

177 FOSSIL CLIFFS

At low tide, if you walk along the cliffs between New Brighton Beach and Capitola, you will see above you exposed sandstone and siltstone that were deposited 3 to 5 million years ago. Embedded in that sandstone and siltstone are layers of fossil beds that were part of a continental shelf 30 to 150 feet under water. Within those layers,

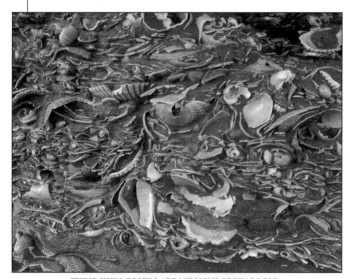

THESE SHELL FOSSILS ARE MILLIONS OF YEARS OLD.

more than 60 species of fossils have been found, including many varieties of clam and snail shells. If you look carefully along the cliff wall, you will see distinct layers of shell fossils, 1 to 3 feet thick, some visible for hundreds of feet along the exposed surface of the cliff. An even easier way to see the fossils is just to look down at the rocks and boulders at the base of the cliffs. Many of those rocks contain dense concentrations of fossils that stand out beautifully against the gray of the sandstone. (Please note that it is illegal to collect fossils from the beach.) Remember not to stand directly below the cliffs due to the danger of erosion and falling rocks, and also pay attention to the changing tides.

PACIFIC MIGRATIONS INTERACTIVE MAP

Dominating the entrance to the Pacific Migrations visitor center at New Brighton State Beach is a bright and colorful 50-square-foot wall map that offers a rare view of the entire Pacific Basin, from the coasts of North and South America to the islands and waterways of Asia, Southeast Asia, Australia and Antarctica. What makes the map most remarkable are the hundreds of LED lights that illuminate the migration patterns of some notable local creatures. Press a button and see the 10,000-mile route that gray whales make on their annual trek between the Bering Sea and Baja California. Press another button and discover the places monarch butterflies

LIGHTS MARK MIGRATIONS

go every fall and winter to escape the cold. Press yet another button and chart the unbelievable flight of the sooty shearwaters, who travel up to 40,000 miles a year to and from New Zealand and the North Pacific Ocean. Press a final button to see the powerful Pacific currents that aided early sailors and helped bring human immigrants to the California coast. The theme of migration from one country or region to another is reinforced throughout the visitor center, with displays on the Chinese fishing village at the base of the bluff (known as China Beach or China Cove), the early ranchos and resorts of the New Brighton area, artifacts from the summer cabins at nearby Pot Belly Beach and stories of the native Ohlone people. The center is open during the summer season with limited hours, so it is always best to call the state park to confirm the schedule.

■ **The Pacific Migrations visitor center is located near the main entrance to the New Brighton State Beach campground.**

AN AMAZING INTERACTIVE PACIFIC OCEAN MAP

LAND OF THE MEDICINE BUDDHA

Land of the Medicine Buddha is a Tibetan Buddhist center and spiritual retreat located several miles above Soquel on more than 100 acres of meadows and densely forested land. This is a tranquil place, designed for contemplation, and the public is welcome to enjoy the hiking trails and the many holy objects on display throughout the grounds and in the meditation halls. While you are there, here are some points of interest to explore.

■ **Land of the Medicine Buddha is located at 5800 Prescott Road, Soquel.**

8 VERSES LOOP TRAIL AND THE ENCHANTED FOREST

The easy 8 Verses Loop Trail is designed especially for meditation and reflection and will take you approximately 45 minutes to complete. Eight Dharma quotes are affixed on trees spaced along the trail, each with an accompanying commentary by the Dalai Lama. At every verse, there is a bench for resting and contemplation. Halfway through the loop, you will have the option of taking a side trail into the Enchanted Forest for a much longer hike of about 2.5 hours. Here the canopy changes quickly from a mixture of vegetation to a quiet redwood forest of towering trees and soft soil.

THE PRAYER WHEEL

There are several prayer wheels at Land of the Medicine Buddha. The largest and most impressive is the wheel at the main entrance that was built to commemorate the 2001 visit of His Holiness the Dalai Lama. It is brightly painted in gold, blue, yellow and red. Prayer wheels are believed to send healing and peace through the power of the prayers and mantras within the wheel. A nearby sign suggests you spin the wheel in a clockwise direction to "Send out good intentions for the Happiness of all beings!"

GIANT GOLDEN BUDDHA

Perhaps the most impressive artwork you will see at Land of the Medicine Buddha is the giant golden Buddha. This seated Buddha is two stories tall and reaches to the ceiling of the Wish Fulfilling Temple mausoleum. The temple is decorated with many detailed and colorful paintings, including a series depicting the life story of the Buddha.

GOLDEN BUDDHA IN THE WISH FULFILLING TEMPLE

THE SKYBALLS

Giant blue spheres seemingly come out of nowhere and appear to be rolling down a steep hill on the edge of Anna Jean Cummings Park in Soquel. These four 8-foot-diameter spheres were created in 2001 by Steve Gillman and Katherine Keefer, who are known for creating site-specific artwork for communities. The concrete spheres are painted sky-blue and their size, unusual color, and cascading hillside location create a surprisingly fun and mysterious impression. While the spheres are officially called Skyballs, locals often refer to Anna Jean Cummings Park with the less dignified nickname, "Blue Ball Park." The 95-acre park is built on two levels: the lower part has a wonderful children's playground and picnic area, while the upper level has soccer and softball fields surrounded by a half-mile walking and jogging path. Above the park is "Killer Hill," a steep trail often used for training cross-country runners. The park is named for Anna Jean Cummings, founder of the Land Trust of Santa Cruz County.

■ **The park is located in Soquel, just past the Soquel High School at 461 Old San Jose Road.**

THESE GIANT BLUE SPHERES CREATE A SURREAL LANDSCAPE.

REDWOOD VILLAGE

Hidden in a redwood grove in Aptos is a cluster of small cabins in a fairy tale setting. Each cabin is different: some are shingled, others are made of clapboard or board and batten, and one is even made of logs with peeling bark. One especially unusual cabin features a tower entry shaped like the base of a giant redwood tree. Called Redwood Village, the 13 cabins were built in 1928 by William Parker as one of California's first motels. Although the 1989 Loma Prieta earthquake destroyed some of the unique masonry chimneys, the wishing well and a fishpond, the village still has the Hansel and Gretel character that is its charm. The motel was popular for many years, although for a time during World War II, it was rented to

A COTTAGE ENTRANCE

families of servicemen training in Watsonville and at Fort Ord. After the war, it was again a motel for honeymooners and other regular visitors until it was sold in 1974. Today, Redwood Village houses offices and shops.

■ **Redwood Village is located at 9099 Soquel Drive, Aptos.**

COTTAGES IN REDWOOD VILLAGE

182 CABRILLO GALLERY

With 1,400 square feet of exhibit space, the Cabrillo College Art Gallery is one of the largest college galleries on the Central Coast and is widely respected throughout the state. Each year the gallery hosts six exhibits, three each during the spring and fall semesters, including an annual exhibition highlighting the works of students in Cabrillo College studio art classes. Up to 200 paintings, photographs, sculptures and jewelry pieces have

ADMISSION TO THIS WONDERFUL GALLERY IS FREE.

been displayed during the student shows. Although the gallery focuses on national and international artists, it also often features Bay Area artists, including Cabrillo College art department staff and faculty. The gallery is open on weekdays during the spring and fall semesters.

■ **Cabrillo Gallery is located in the center of campus beneath the library in Room 1002. Cabrillo College is located at 6500 Soquel Drive, Aptos.**

183 FINDING OUR PAST

In a community of unusual public art installations, the award-winning Finding Our Past, by Susana Arias, is one of the most extraordinary. Created in 1996, this faux archaeological site is comprised of two massive ground-level sculptures about 20 by

FAUX FOSSILS AND ARTIFACTS

80 feet, installed on each side of the Bay/Porter Street exit underpass off Highway 1. It is designed to look like an active archeological dig that has uncovered both historical artifacts such as mortars, arrowheads and old mining tools, and paleontological materials such as whale bones and shark teeth. You can enjoy the sculpture both for its large-scale representation of a roped-off grid-style archaeological site and for the exacting detail of the many individual artifacts on display. Arias was honored by both Caltrans and the California Archaeological Society for this intriguing work of public art. Its under the freeway location means that many people pass by the artwork, but only a few manage to stop and see it. You should consider being one of them. To get to it, you will need to park in one of the many business parking lots on either the Soquel or Capitola side of the freeway underpass and walk back.

■ **Finding Our Past is located at the Bay/Porter Street exit underpass off Highway 1.**

APTOS HISTORY MUSEUM

The long history of the Aptos area—from its Native American beginnings through the Loma Prieta earthquake—is wonderfully presented in the small but fascinating Aptos History Museum. Created through the efforts of John and Karen Hibble, the museum contains artifacts, photographs and memorabilia focused on Aptos Village, Rio del Mar, Seacliff and Seascape. Particularly interesting are the chronological displays of local history juxtaposed against a timeline of significant world events.

■ **The Aptos History Museum is located at 7605-B Old Dominion Court, Aptos, next to the Aptos Chamber of Commerce.**

---

184 OHLONE TULE BOAT

Hanging from the ceiling of the Aptos History Museum is a life-sized replica of a one-person tule boat known as a *kanon* in the Rumsien Ohlone language. For thousands of years, the Ohlone people navigated local waterways using boats woven from tule plants. Tules (also called bulrushes) are commonly seen in California along the edges of lakes, ponds and freshwater marshes. The fibrous,

A REPLICA OF A ONE-PERSON OHLONE CANOE CALLED A *KANON*

grasslike plants are tall, tough and flexible and, because they are lightweight and water repellent, they make excellent boat building material. In September 2006, museum volunteers who were under the direction of Linda Yamane, a well-known local Rumsien Ohlone artist and weaver, gathered tules from Corcoran Lagoon in Capitola and dried them for about 5 weeks. They then created a 14-foot-long historically accurate Ohlone canoe. If you're in the museum during one of their many educational presentations, you might get lucky and see the curator lower the boat for a close-up view. At a nearby display, you can also see an extensive collection of Ohlone tools, artifacts and illustrations documenting early life in the mid-county area.

185 THE PINK MAIDEN

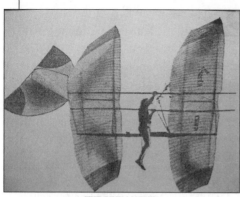

THE *PINK MAIDEN*

If you regularly drive past Waddell Creek on Highway 1, chances are you have seen hang gliders soaring above the cliffs. But not many people know that the town of Aptos was the location of some of the world's first public exhibitions proving that a fixed-wing, heavier-than-air craft was capable of carrying a person in controlled flight. The Aptos History Museum has a wonderful display of photographs, newspaper articles and memorabilia of those early flights, including a replica of the 3.5-foot-long *Pink Maiden*, a prototype glider with wings covered in pink silk. The *Pink Maiden* was designed by John J. Montgomery and flown off the railroad trestle at La Selva Beach to test his theories of flight. This small prototype later became the design for the full-sized craft used in flights by aeronaut Daniel John Maloney. In March 1905, he and a 38-pound tandem wing glider designed by Montgomery were sent aloft by a hot air balloon on multiple flights above Aptos. On his longest flight, Maloney was cut loose at 3,000 feet and glided in circles for 18 minutes before landing in a field near Manresa Beach. The replica of the *Pink Maiden* hangs from the ceiling of the museum, ready to soar.

186 FIRST HIGH ALTITUDE AEROPLANE FLIGHTS MARKER

In March 2005, a small monument was dedicated on the 100th anniversary of the three soaring flights made by Daniel John Maloney in the glider designed by John J. Montgomery. The centennial marker sits in an open field near the former Leonard Ranch in Seascape where the flights took place. Look up and imagine a hot air balloon dropping a glider from 3,000 feet above this field. The bronze plaque honors Montgomery as the "Father of Basic Flying" for his early and famous flying exploits. Although he has been largely forgotten, you can honor him with a quick visit to this simple memorial.

■ The High Altitude Aeroplane Flights Marker is located at the end of Dolphin Drive in Seascape.

MONUMENT HONORS
JOHN J. MONTGOMERY.

187 BAY VIEW HOTEL

Partially hidden behind one of the largest magnolia trees you will ever see is the magnificent Bay View Hotel, the oldest operating hotel in Santa Cruz County. Joseph Arano, one of Aptos' earliest settlers, built the Victorian-Italianate hotel in 1878. The rail line connecting Santa Cruz and Pajaro Valley had been completed in 1876 and Arano's plan was to take advantage of this strategic site in Aptos Village, which was growing rapidly in support of the nearby lumber industry. The elegant hotel was first named the Anchor House and offered 28 rooms and formal gardens. The marble fireplace mantels were from France and the furniture handcrafted in Spain. Soon renamed Bay View Hotel, the business remained in the Arano family until 1942. The new owners planned to tear the hotel down but fortunately decided to move the building instead. The structure was jacked up and moved on rollers 118 feet into the original formal gardens and situated directly behind the old magnolia tree. Over the years, the hotel has been modernized and passed through the hands of several owners. Stories of ghost sightings and furniture that moves mysteriously by itself have

fueled rumors of spirits haunting the old hotel. Despite this, the Bay View Hotel continues to operate as a bed and breakfast inn and is a beautiful centerpiece to Aptos Village. It is worth a visit to admire its elaborate architecture.

■ **The Bay View Hotel is located at 8041 Soquel Drive, Aptos.**

BAY VIEW HOTEL WAS BUILT ON THE RAIL LINE BETWEEN SANTA CRUZ AND PAJARO VALLEY.

188 DOUG KIRBY SWALE

THE SWALE WAS DEDICATED IN OCTOBER 2008.

Starting near Sumner Avenue and Dry Creek Road in Rio del Mar is a short but scenic path that travels past redwood and eucalyptus trees and under the railroad trestle toward Hidden Beach. It is named in honor of nearby resident Doug Kirby, who spent more than 20 years clearing brush and removing diseased trees from this onetime overgrown and poison oak–infested swale. Now graced with new trees and native shrubs, the Doug Kirby Swale is a tribute to the volunteer spirit of a man with a vision.

■ **The Doug Kirby Swale is located off Sumner Avenue in Rio del Mar.**

189 SOARING SEAGULL SCULPTURE

Hidden in plain sight, in the center of the traffic island that separates Rio del Mar Boulevard and Clubhouse Drive, is a slender, soaring, 14-foot-tall steel shaft supporting a seagull in flight. It was designed by sculptor Joseph Spencer and erected in 1976 to honor longtime Rio del Mar resident and community volunteer Tom Whaley. Though it stands unnoticed by the thousands of cars that pass by every day, this simple and graceful piece of art clearly deserves a closer look. You can also see a small scale model of the sculpture on display in the Aptos History Museum.

■ **The Soaring Seagull sculpture is located in a traffic island on Rio del Mar Boulevard.**

WHERE IS THIS SEAGULL HEADED?

GLAUM EGG RANCH
EGG VENDING MACHINE

Take a drive into the country to buy fresh eggs from the egg vending machine at the Glaum Egg Ranch. A few dollars will buy you a flat of eggs and a musical puppet show that changes seasonally. The curtain goes up and costumed hens and chicks dance and cluck to the music while your flat of eggs glides out of the vending slot like magic. A family business since the 1920s and now in its third generation, Glaum's eggs are sold at many local stores. But it's a special treat to buy them at the ranch from the egg vending machine. You'll want to buy a second flat just to see the show again! As you drive to leave the ranch, a cheery sign wishes "Have an EGGcellent day!"

■ **Glaum Egg Ranch is located at 3100 Valencia Road, Aptos.**

DANCING CHICKS PERFORM IN THE EGG VENDING MACHINE.

VALENCIA HALL AND POST OFFICE

Valencia Hall and Valencia Post Office are situated on a narrow and winding country road outside of Aptos. Built in the early 1880s, these are the only surviving structures of the once thriving lumber town of Valencia, home to hundreds of sawmill workers and their families. Frederick Hihn was a German immigrant and prosperous entrepreneur who made millions from his lumber and other local business endeavors. Valencia, the company town for Hihn's sawmill operations on Valencia Creek, was built to produce 70,000 board feet of lumber per day. The heart of the community was Valencia Hall, built by Hihn as a community meeting place, for church services and for school commencements. After operations at the Valencia Mill ceased in 1902, the area became a thriving apple-growing region, and picturesque orchards and redwood trees still surround the property. These simple white clapboard buildings have been restored and are now a Santa Cruz County park used for weddings and other functions.

■ **Valencia Hall and Post Office are located at 2555 Valencia Road, Aptos.**

VALENCIA HALL

THE FOREST OF NISENE MARKS

The Forest of Nisene Marks is a 10,000-acre undeveloped state park that was home to large-scale lumbering operations from 1880 to 1920. It has more than 40 miles of hiking trails and is very popular with runners, hikers and mountain bikers.

■ **The Forest of Nisene Marks is located up Aptos Creek Road near Aptos Village.**

192 ADVOCATE TREE

Over 1,000 years old and 253 feet tall, the Advocate Tree is one of the largest redwoods in the Forest of Nisene Marks State Park. It has an 18-foot-tall "goosepen" (the wide-open scar caused by fires that burn into a tree's heartwood), which is probably one of the reasons it was spared the axe when much of the rest of the forest was being logged. This huge leaning tower, 39 feet in circumference, is located along the Old Growth Loop Trail, near the entrance kiosk to the park. Along the 1.1-mile trail, which is quite steep in places, you will also find the Twisted Grove with its unusual-shaped redwoods. To get to the Old Growth Loop, you need to cross Aptos Creek. Be aware that there is no bridge from November through April and, in winter, the creek can be impassable or require fording on slippery rocks or logs.

THE HUGE GOOSEPEN
PROBABLY SAVED THIS GIANT
FROM LOGGING.

■ **The Old Growth Loop Trail is near the entrance kiosk.**

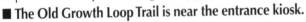

193 BUDDHA UNDER THE BRIDGE

The Buddha stands surrounded by photographs, flowers and small offerings. Over the years he has been dislocated by storms and vandalism, yet always returns to provide hope and comfort to those in need. You can find him under the picturesque Mill Pond Trail Bridge (also known as Buddha Bridge) in the Forest of Nisene Marks State Park. To get there, take the Loma Prieta Grade Trail past the Porter House Site where you will find historical markers and displays of the home and cottage buildings that once stood there. Just past the Porter House Site, turn right onto Mill Pond Trail and head down the trail to the arched bridge crossing the creek. The shrine rests under the west side of the bridge.

MANY PEOPLE LEAVE PHOTOS
OR IMAGES OF LOVED ONES.

■ **The Buddha Bridge is on the Loma Prieta Grade Trail, past the Porter House Site.**

EPICENTER OF THE QUAKE OF 1989

There is no giant crevasse, no forest of toppled trees, just a sign on a path next to a babbling creek. On October 17, 1989, at 5:04 p.m., a magnitude 6.9 earthquake struck the San Francisco and Monterey Bay regions. Known as the Loma Prieta earthquake, it killed 63 people, injured thousands and left many more thousands homeless. The epicenter of the quake is located in the Forest of Nisene Marks State Park along the peaceful Aptos Creek Trail. In the immediate aftermath of the quake there were fallen trees, exposed cliffs where boulders fell and giant fissures in the

earth. The forest has grown back and most of the obvious signs of the quake are hard to discern without expert guidance. But now thousands of people make the pilgrimage along what was a rarely used trail to pay their respects to the power of the earth. The 2.1-mile hike to the epicenter takes about 45 to 60 minutes from the Porter Family Picnic Area parking lot. En route to Aptos Creek Trail along Aptos Creek Fire Road, you may want to stop at the interpretive panel at the Loma Prieta Sawmill site or at the display showcasing the

TO FULLY APPRECIATE IT, YOU HAD TO BE THERE. OR NOT.

Incline Railroad Line, a steam-powered "bull donkey" that lowered redwood lumber 600 feet down the mountainside. Once on the single-track Aptos Creek Trail to the epicenter, you will have to scramble over rocks to cross the creek twice (easier in the late summer). You will see lots of redwoods, firs, willows, alders and many types of ferns before you arrive at the epicenter. Look around at the steep cliffs above you and imagine what it would have been like to be here on that October evening.

■ **The epicenter of the 1989 Loma Prieta earthquake is located along the Aptos Creek Trail, off the Porter Family Picnic Area parking lot in the Forest of Nisene Marks State Park.**

SOUTH COUNTY: WATSONVILLE & LA SELVA BEACH

South County includes La Selva Beach, a small residential community perched on the bluffs overlooking Monterey Bay, and the historic City of Watsonville, center of Santa Cruz County's agricultural heartland. Here are historic buildings, museums, the Santa Cruz County Fairgrounds, and many points of interest that focus on the area's agricultural history.

FRUIT CRATE LABEL MURALS

Local fruit crate labels are a colorful and unique piece of Pajaro Valley's agricultural heritage, and you can see them on display as large murals on the sides of buildings in downtown Watsonville. In the early 20th century, the apple industry was booming in Watsonville and competition was fierce. Each company wanted to be noticed, so crate labels were used as a form of advertising. Artists were hired to create colorful labels with eye-catching imagery. In the Pajaro Valley, early apple growers such as White Star, Butterfly, Mission Bell

MISSION BELL LABEL MURAL

and Martinelli were among the first to use crate labels. Eventually, hundreds of labels were produced by farmers throughout Watsonville and the Pajaro Valley. By the 1950s, cardboard boxes replaced the labels and a beautiful art form was lost. The City of Watsonville and private individuals have funded the Historic Label Art Mural Project and engaged artists to paint exact replicas of the original labels as super-sized murals downtown. Take a walking tour to see the murals, using the mural guide and map published by the city and available online.

■ **The murals are on building walls in the heart of downtown Watsonville.**

FRUIT CRATE LABEL MURALS ON A UNION STREET BUILDING

LA SELVA BEACH

La Selva Beach is a charming community above Monterey Bay and well worth a visit for some local sights and spectacular views. The land was a Jesuit retreat in 1925 when enterprising real estate developer D. W. Batchelor purchased it. Some say Batchelor personally drew up the plans for his new town while sitting on a log near the site of the current La Selva Beach Clubhouse. Honoring his Scottish heritage, Batchelor named his town Rob Roy, after the legendary highland chief, and gave all the streets Scottish names. Batchelor built the roads, water and sewage systems and brought in electricity. He set aside land for a church, school, playground and several parks before he began to sell lots. By 1935, a number of lots still remained unsold and Batchelor sold these to Edward Burghard of Los Angeles, who hoped to attract Hollywood celebrities to the area. Burghard renamed the community La Selva Beach (La Selva means "jungle" in Spanish) and gave the streets new Spanish names.

■ **La Selva Beach is located off San Andreas Road.**

196 THE PALM TREES

MEXICAN FAN PALMS IN LA SELVA BEACH

Among the first things you'll notice when you arrive at La Selva Beach are the rows of thin, tall palm trees that line both sides of Playa Boulevard, the town's main thoroughfare. The trees are Mexican fan palms, more aptly known as skyduster palms. These palms often reach heights of 80 to 100 feet. The palms in La Selva Beach are, sadly, nearing the end of their natural lives.

■ **The palms are on Playa Boulevard, La Selva Beach.**

197 VIEW FROM THE BLUFFS

On a clear day you can see for miles from the bluffs at La Selva Beach, one of the best vantage points in the county for uninterrupted beach views in both directions. This perfect spot puts you high above Monterey Bay, and you can rest on a bench

near the eucalyptus grove and watch the waves roll in for miles. If the evening is clear, there is no better spot to watch the sun slip into the bay at sunset. This is the place to find inspiration if you need it or to be humbled by the beauty of Monterey Bay.

■ **The bluffs are off Vista Drive, La Selva Beach.**

VIEW TOWARD SANTA CRUZ FROM LA SELVA BEACH BLUFFS

198 RAILROAD TRESTLE

The railroad trestle at La Selva Beach is a local landmark. A wooden trestle spanned this gully until the area's original developer helped convince Southern Pacific Railroad to replace the old wooden trestle with the steel structure still in use today. Up to the mid-1930s, four trains carrying passengers, newspapers and freight arrived daily at the local station, with an extra train arriving on Sunday.

■ **You'll get the best view of the trestle from the bluffs at the end of Playa Boulevard, La Selva Beach.**

VIEW OF THE TRESTLE FROM THE BLUFFS AT LA SELVA BEACH

DECO GAS STATION

The Watsonville Auto Center mascot is a tiny former Flying A gas station built in 1938 and moved to its current location in 2007. True to its Streamline Moderne architectural style, the building celebrates the Machine Age. You will notice that its main feature is a small, tiered tower that resembles a screw head. Large panes of glass provide a clear view of the kiosk interior. A canopy, which at one time sheltered patrons and their automobiles at the pump, extends neatly to one side. The building is clad entirely in metal and is painted a crisp white with red stripes. Atop the structure sits a ball light that, along with neon tower illumination, gives the diminutive building a grand presence after dark.

■ **The little gas station is at 998 Main Street, at the corner of Auto Center Drive, Watsonville.**

FORMER FLYING A STREAMLINE MODERNE GAS STATION

200 ST. PATRICK'S CHURCH

The dramatic architecture of St. Patrick's Catholic Church makes an impressive landmark at the entrance to Watsonville. While you might think the English Gothic Revival brick building is old, it was, in fact, completely rebuilt after the Loma Prieta earthquake damaged the original 1903 church building. The old building, designed by renowned local architect William H. Weeks, survived the 1906 earthquake relatively unscathed; but on October 17, 1989, the Loma Prieta earthquake caused serious damage. At first, the parish intended to repair and retrofit the building; however, the cost to do so proved to be too high. After much debate, the parish decided to demolish and rebuild the church to look exactly as it had before the earthquake. The building was carefully dismantled and many of its features were saved for use in the replica, including the old stained-glass windows and the original doors. The cornerstone was laid on St. Patrick's Day 1994, and today this beautiful building stands again, with many lovely original elements intact. Visit the inside of the building and take a look at the beautiful windows depicting various saints. You will also want to study the lovely interior woodwork, especially the ornate ceiling spandrels and the Stations of the Cross woodcarvings.

■ **St. Patrick's Catholic Church is located at the intersection of Main Street and Freedom Boulevard, Watsonville.**

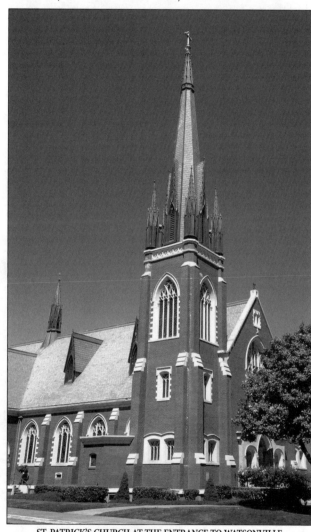

ST. PATRICK'S CHURCH AT THE ENTRANCE TO WATSONVILLE

WATSONVILLE PLAZA

For over 150 years, Watsonville Plaza has hosted concerts, street fairs, political protests and patriotic celebrations. Situated in the heart of the downtown historic district, it is a quiet oasis of grass and ornamental trees, crisscrossed with pathways and dotted with benches. The plaza was donated to the people of Watsonville by the heirs of the prominent landholder, Don Sebastian Rodriguez, in 1860. In the center of the plaza is a 23-foot-diameter stone bandstand designed by William H. Weeks and built by Granite Rock Company in 1906. Make sure you wander in for a closer look, because embedded into the stone work are four cast-concrete gargoyles representing music and entertainment. The gargoyles are playing flutes and putting on masks. The plaza is also known for its 1880 granite fountain, donated

THIS BANDSTAND GARGOYLE HOLDS A MASK TO ITS FACE.

by the Butterfly Social Club, and for a drinking fountain originally donated by the Women's Christian Temperance Union in 1893 and modernized in 1913. An 1899 field gun from the Spanish American War sits on the southwest corner of the plaza, and nearby on a pedestal is a bust of George Washington by sculptor Michelle Armitage. Watsonville Plaza is included in the "Walking and Driving Tour of Historic Main Street," published by the City of Watsonville Community Development Department and available online. Small town plazas are an increasingly rare part of the American urban landscape, and this one is especially nice.

■ **The Watsonville Plaza is located at the intersection of Main and East Beach Streets, Watsonville.**

AN 1899 FIELD GUN FROM THE SPANISH AMERICAN WAR

THE CANNON THAT PROCLAIMED CALIFORNIA STATEHOOD

As part of the Compromise of 1850, California was admitted to the Union on September 9, 1850, as a free state (where slavery was prohibited). On October 18, as the Pacific Mail Steamship Company's S.S. *Oregon* headed into San Francisco Bay, its cannon fired what is purported to be the first salute proclaiming California statehood. According to historian Betty Lewis, the City of Watsonville borrowed that same cannon from San Francisco in 1876 to help celebrate the nation's centennial and it was never returned. After being long forgotten, the cannon was refurbished and remounted in 1922 for the City of Watsonville by the Native Sons of the Golden West and now sits in Watsonville Plaza. It is a small but important part of California history. You may want to honor it with a visit on Admission Day (September 9) or anytime.

■ **The cannon is located in Watsonville Plaza, at the intersection of Main and East Beach Streets, Watsonville.**

YOU CAN WALK UP AND TOUCH THIS HISTORIC CANNON IN WATSONVILLE PLAZA.

CALIFORNIA AGRICULTURAL WORKERS' HISTORY CENTER

On the second floor of the Watsonville Public Library is the California Agricultural Workers' History Center. It is a self-contained research room that houses archival material focused on the history of the people who have worked in the fields and orchards of California, from farmworkers, fruit pickers and apricot cutters to cannery workers and tractor drivers. The center documents and honors their lives, working conditions and labor struggles.

■ The California Agricultural Workers' History Center is located on the second floor of the Watsonville Public Library, 275 Main Street, Watsonville.

203 BY THE STRENGTH OF OUR HANDS

Directly outside the center is a 40-foot-long, glass-enclosed exhibit illustrating the history of agricultural workers within the Monterey Bay area. By the Strength of Our Hands/Por La Fuerza de Nuestras Manos was designed and curated by Charles Prentiss and Nikki Silva. Using old books and photographs, engravings, and fruit and vegetable displays, the bilingual exhibit provides a visual introduction to the multicultural history of our local agricultural workers. While immigrants from central and southern Mexico currently make up the largest part of the workforce,

THIS EXHIBIT HONORS OUR AGRICULTURAL
WORKERS AND THEIR FAMILIES.

historically, our agricultural workers have come from all over the world. Chinese immigrants dominated from the 1860s to 1890s. The Japanese arrived in the 1880s; the Croatian migration peaked between 1900 and World War I. Filipinos came in the 1920s and dust bowl migrants in the 1930s. All of those groups, plus the Portuguese, Irish, Italian, Swiss and African Americans are highlighted in the exhibit, along with fascinating historical summaries of the Bracero Program years after World War II and the labor unrest of the 1970s and 1980s. A short visit will dramatically increase your understanding and appreciation of the men, women and children who are the key part of our local agricultural history.

204 ARTICHOKE PICKERS MURAL

THE MURAL IS BASED ON A 1935 STUDY BY ARTIST HENRIETTA SHORE.

The bonus feature of the California Agricultural Workers' History Center is the mural surrounding the exhibit. It depicts migrant workers harvesting artichokes near Elkhorn Slough during the Great Depression. The mural wraps around three sides of the exhibit and its compelling images and bold colors brighten the entire second floor of the Watsonville Public Library. The mural was recreated using designs from a 1935 mural study by Carmel artist Henrietta Shore. A close friend of Edward Weston and greatly influenced by Diego Rivera and other Mexican artists, Shore was renowned for her modernist floral paintings, which were often compared to those by Georgia O'Keeffe. Four of her original murals can be seen at the Downtown Santa Cruz Post Office (see page 16).

205 1905 GRANDFATHER CLOCK

In 1905 the Benevolent and Protective Order of Elks presented the then-brand-new Carnegie Library in Watsonville with a Seth Thomas hall clock, known more fondly as a grandfather clock. At over 100 years of age, it is still beautiful and works perfectly. Its carved-oak case has a shell motif and the wonderfully ornate clockface has a lunar dial showing the phases of the moon. You can see the weight-driven pendulum through the glass door of the tall case. Time your visit for the top of the hour to hear the clock chime.

■ **Located inside the Agricultural Workers' History Center.**

THIS SETH THOMAS CLOCK IS OVER 7 FEET TALL.

206 MANSION HOUSE

Main Street in downtown Watsonville is lined with historic buildings, many of which have informative signs on the sidewalk explaining their history. Take a walking tour of Main Street starting at one of the oldest buildings on the street, the Mansion House, built in 1871. In its day, this three-story redwood building was the best hotel

MANSION HOUSE, BUILT 1871

in town. In fact, President Ulysses S. Grant stayed here. The hotel originally offered 65 rooms on the second and third floors; in 1900 a room cost $2 a night. The ground floor had a billiard room and bar, dining room, reading room, office parlor and three stores. The Mansion House has a beautiful mansard roof and originally had a wide front porch with a veranda above. The building was moved from the corner of Main and Beach Streets in 1913 to make room for the new and more modern Lettunich

Building next door. The Mansion House was jacked up and lowered onto 100-foot-long log rollers to make the 110-foot move. In 1978, the building was scheduled for demolition but was saved by the Pajaro Valley Historical Association.

■ **You will find the Mansion House at 418 Main Street, Watsonville.**

207 LETTUNICH SKYSCRAPER

The four-story Lettunich Building was called a "skyscraper" when it was built in 1914, its height made possible through construction of steel and reinforced concrete. The impressive building had every modern convenience including electricity, steam heat and water, and the exciting and new Cutter Patent Mail Chute. Twenty-seven offices on

three upper floors were reachable by electric elevator. Owners Mateo and M. N. Lettunich were prominent orchardists and owners of Pajaro Valley's largest fruit-packing business. Perhaps in recognition of this, brightly colored ornamentation over the entrance of the building depicts fruits of the Pajaro Valley. Look for the friezes showing a bear and a winged Mercury.

■ **Located at 406 Main Street at the corner of Main and East Beach Street, Watsonville.**

FRUITS OF PAJARO VALLEY ADORN THE ENTRANCE.

CHIEF GENE FRIEND FIRE MUSEUM

In 1915 Watsonville purchased its first motorized fire engine, a Seagrave Auto Fire Truck that could pump 750 gallons of water per minute. A special bond was issued by the City of Watsonville to raise the $10,000 needed to buy the engine that came to be known affectionately as "Old Buck." Old Buck stayed on the job until her last fire on May 7, 1945, during which she pumped steadily for 6 hours. In 1958, she was sold to the City of Freedom.

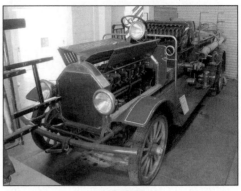

OLD BUCK

At last, too old and outdated for service, Old Buck was moved to the Firehouse Restaurant on Cannery Row in Monterey where she became a tourist attraction. Eventually she was returned to her rightful home in the Fire Station in Watsonville. You can visit her, and several engines purchased later, at the Chief Gene Friend Fire Museum in the historic Fire Station 1 building. They are on display along with numerous historical photographs, equipment and other items from firefighting history in Watsonville. Call before your visit to check museum hours.

■ **The Chief Gene Friend Fire Museum is at 105 Second Street, Watsonville.**

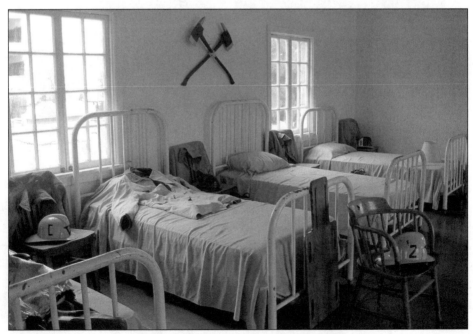

HISTORIC WATSONVILLE FIRE STATION DORMITORY

209 BOCKIUS-ORR HOUSE AND GARDENS

Step back in time to the late 1800s and experience Watsonville life at its finest. The Italianate-Victorian Bockius-Orr House sits 200 feet back from East Beach Street on a magnificently landscaped lot with century-old coastal live oaks, crepe myrtle and boxwood hedges. Designed by Alex Chalmers and built for Godfrey Bockius in 1870, the house is on the National Register of Historic Houses and is now home to the Pajaro Valley Historical Association. The parlor, main reception room, bedroom and kitchen are open to the public and display period furniture and antiques. The association also owns an extensive collection of textiles and men's and women's fashions from the 1860s onward and these are exhibited in the rear parlor on a rotating basis throughout the year. Behind the house is a rose garden, flowering shrubs, an English walnut tree and a rare dawn redwood. The Pajaro Valley Historical Association also maintains the Snyder Archive, which has a treasure trove of historical documents, photographs, manuscripts, oral histories and other artifacts essential for anyone doing historical or genealogical research about families and businesses in the Pajaro Valley. Since visiting hours are limited to a few midweek days, be sure to call ahead.

■ **Located at 332 East Beach Street, Watsonville.**

THE BOCKIUS-ORR HOUSE WAS DONATED TO THE HISTORICAL ASSOCIATION IN 1993 BY ZOE ANN ORR MARCUS.

210 THE SQUARE GRAND PIANO

Even though they were the most popular piano sold in America for over a century, few people have seen a square grand piano. Even fewer have seen one as rare and as beautifully embellished as the piano that sits in the living room of the Bockius-Orr House. Over 7 feet wide and about 4 feet deep, the ornately carved rosewood piano cabinet sits on four legs, with strings running from left to right. Sometimes known as a box grand, square grand pianos were built until the end of the 19th century when the development of upright pianos made them obsolete. This Haines Brothers square case grand piano is believed to have been manufactured in 1858 and was originally purchased by Claus Spreckels for his home in Soquel. The keys are made of ebony and mother-of-pearl, and the piano case has been inlaid with an intricate mother-of-pearl floral design. It is another great reason to visit the Bockius-Orr House.

A SIMILAR HAINES BROTHERS PIANO IS IN THE DE YOUNG MUSEUM IN SAN FRANCISCO.

211 VOLCK MUSEUM AND TANK HOUSE

This tiny museum, part of the Pajaro Valley Historical Association complex, is the original carriage house for the 1870 Bockius-Orr House. Today, the museum houses artifacts from the early years of Watsonville including old household appliances, tools and small displays of classroom, general store and drugstore paraphernalia. It sits adjacent to the architecturally stunning Tank House, which pumped and stored water for the house and farm. Visitors to the Bockius-Orr House can tour the Volck Museum on request.

THE 35-FOOT-TALL TANK HOUSE IS THE LAST ONE IN TOWN.

PAJARO VALLEY ARTS COUNCIL GALLERY

One of the finest art galleries in the county is located in Watsonville in a turn-of-the-last-century Victorian bungalow designed by architect William H. Weeks. Sponsored by the Pajaro Valley Arts Council (PVAC), the gallery reflects their mission to "bring the community together through the arts." Hosting visual art exhibits with creative themes that highlight local cultural and environmental issues, the gallery, which first opened in 1986, inspires artists to create specific pieces for the many rotating shows. The gallery's strong connection to the local art and environmental communities means that they attract some of the best artists in the county. Their new shows are always worth a visit.

■ **The Pajaro Valley Arts Council Gallery is located at 37 Sudden Street, Watsonville.**

THE PVAC GALLERY BUILDING WAS DESIGNED BY ARCHITECT WILLIAM H. WEEKS IN 1903.

THE SCULPTURE GARDEN AT SIERRA AZUL NURSERY

LINDBERG AND THOMAS' GIANT DRAGONFLY FLOATS ABOVE THE GARDEN.

Every year, from the end of May through October, approximately 100 sculptures by dozens of local artists are put on display in a beautiful 2-acre coastal garden near the county fairgrounds. Sponsored by the Pajaro Valley Arts Council and hosted by Sierra Azul Nursery, the sculptures include both small and towering works in stone, steel, glass and ceramic. As you wander the garden, you will discover sculptures nestled among a variety of California, Australia, New Zealand and Mediterranean plants, trees and grasses. While the sponsored show happens during the summer and fall, the garden is open year-round, with many works remaining on display. The nursery's permanent collection includes the soaring copper and steel Dragonflies and Mayflies by Scott Lindberg and Cristie Thomas, the recycled agricultural and mechanical steel Crankshaft Finial Pagoda by Magdalena McCann, and the stone-and-steel bench Between Rock and a Hard Space by Takashi Nakagawa.

■ The sculpture garden is located within Sierra Azul Nursery at 2660 East Lake Avenue (Highway 152) across from the Santa Cruz County Fairgrounds in Watsonville.

MAGDALENA MCCANN CREATES ART FROM RECYCLED STEEL.

214 MORRIS TUTTLE MANSION

You can see many fine historic homes in Watsonville, but few can compare with the Morris Tuttle Mansion. The mansion cost $20,000 to build in 1899, with the carpentry alone costing more than $5,000, a staggering amount at the time. Tuttle was one of the leading orchardists in the Pajaro Valley. He was so successful that he hired architect William H. Weeks to design this showcase residence. Weeks was already well known as the architect to the Watsonville wealthy and he ultimately designed many prominent buildings in Santa Cruz County and throughout California. The home Weeks designed for Tuttle was palatial by any measure. Expensive Hungarian ash, oak, cedar, bird's-eye maple and mahogany were used in the interior. The ground floor exterior is built from blocks of granite and Arizona sandstone, perhaps helping this grand building survive the major earthquakes of 1906 and 1989. The mansion was divided into residential apartments in 1939, a property management company purchased it in 1974, and today the mansion is an office building. Stop by and take a closer look.

■ **The Morris Tuttle Mansion is located at 723 East Lake Avenue, Watsonville.**

THE GRAND MORRIS TUTTLE MANSION WAS BUILT IN 1899.

215 VALLEY CHURCH

The striking Romanesque-style Our Lady Help of Christians Valley Catholic Church, popularly known as "Valley Church," stands near the county fairgrounds, surrounded by a historic cemetery that is notable for its many beautiful mausoleums. The church stands on the site of the first house of worship built in the Pajaro Valley. In the mid-1800s, Watsonville was still a tiny community and local Catholics had to travel to Mission San Juan Bautista or Mission Santa Cruz to worship. In 1854, a parcel of land was donated by a local farming family so that a church and cemetery

MAUSOLEUMS IN THE CHURCH CEMETERY

could be built. The new church was built in 1855 and after being enlarged several times, burned to the ground in 1927. The cornerstone of the present fireproof church was laid on May 17, 1928. The Salesian Order of St. John Bosco has ministered the church and nearby school since 1921. Take time to explore the church and cemetery. Inside the church, you will see the large painting, "Our Lady, Help of Christians," the work of Italian painter C. Morgari. This painting is a copy of the original, commissioned in 1868 by St. John Bosco, patron saint of the Salesians, which hangs over the main altar of the Basilica of Our Lady Help of Christians in Turin, Italy.

■ Valley Church is located at 2401 East Lake Avenue, Watsonville.

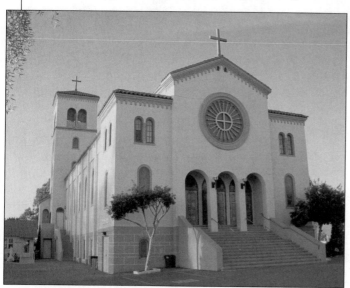

VALLEY CHURCH IS BUILT IN THE ROMANESQUE STYLE.

THE AGRICULTURAL HISTORY PROJECT

Located at the entrance to the Santa Cruz County Fairgrounds in Watsonville, the Agricultural History Project and Museum is home to exhibits and demonstrations that explain in depth the agricultural history of the Central Coast. In several barns and sheds, you'll find more than 10,000 artifacts and an exhaustive collection of antique farm tools including numerous tractors, carriages, appliances, hand tools and much more.

■ **The Agricultural History Project is located at 2601 East Lake Avenue, Watsonville.**

216 CODIGA CENTER AND MUSEUM

The museum features in-depth exhibits of apple, strawberry and artichoke growing, as well as cattle ranching. Photographic displays show how crops and livestock came to the Pajaro Valley and who brought them here. "When Apples Were King" tells the story of the Pajaro Valley apple industry. "Legacy of the Vaqueros" traces cattle from the Mission days to the present. You will also see displays about food preservation and large collections of historic fruit jars and milk bottles. Take a close look at what a kitchen would have been like in the 1920s when food preservation at home was a standard practice.

THIS 1920s-ERA KITCHEN IS ON DISPLAY IN THE CODIGA CENTER AND MUSEUM.

217 PORTER IMPLEMENT SHED

If you'd like to learn how seed was cleaned, corn removed from the cob or apple cider pressed in the old days on the farm, step into the Porter Implement Shed. Here you can see an extensive collection of machines and hand tools that were used to do these and many other farming tasks in the early days of Central Coast agriculture. The implement shed also includes a collection of plows, reapers and planters.

PART OF THE VAST HAND TOOL COLLECTION

218 THE SHOP

The Snyder Building, also known as The Shop, is a large barn full—from top to bottom—of every kind of appliance, carriage and tractor imaginable. Some have been fully restored, others are works in progress, and still others sit rusty and waiting for attention. Don't be surprised to find someone working on a piece of old equipment while you are there.

APPLIANCES, CARRIAGES AND TRACTORS

219 BORINA TRACTOR BARN

This 140-by-40-foot open-air barn houses dozens of vintage restored tractors. Some have well-known names, such as Caterpillar and John Deere, and others are from lesser-known companies, such as Fordson Tractor, established by automobile magnate, Henry Ford. Displays show how the tractor changed farming on the Central Coast.

A SMALL PART OF THE LARGE TRACTOR COLLECTION

RODGERS HOUSE

In 1870 James Rodgers built the Italianate-style farmhouse, now sitting at the entrance to the Santa Cruz County Fairgrounds, for his wife Malvina and their eight children. It was later the family home of Esther Steinbeck Rodgers, sister of famed author John Steinbeck. In 1998, the house was saved from destruction and moved in several pieces to its current location at the fairgrounds for restoration as a museum and for special events. The house is fully furnished, mostly with Rodgers' family furnishings from several generations and with additional personal items including Malvina's Victorian-era wedding dress, and photographs and paintings of members of the Rodgers family, including John Steinbeck. There are also historic photographs of Pajaro Valley. The kitchen is completely equipped with all original fixtures and furniture,

RODGERS HOUSE AT THE SANTA CRUZ COUNTY FAIRGROUNDS

including Esther's curtains, which still hang in the windows. Of special interest in the living room is a rare 360-degree panorama photograph of San Francisco, taken from the Mark Hopkins mansion on Nob Hill in 1877 by famed photographer Eadweard Muybridge, a friend of the Rodgers family. The original of this photograph is in the Library of Congress. Muybridge is well known for his animal locomotion photography, with which he famously proved that all four of a horse's hooves are off the ground at the same time during gallop. You can tour the house during the annual county fair in September or by special arrangement during the rest of the year.

■ **The Rodgers House is located at the entrance of the Santa Cruz County Fairgrounds, 2601 East Lake Avenue, Watsonville.**

A PORTION OF THE 1877 PANORAMA OF SAN FRANCISCO, TAKEN BY EADWEARD MUYBRIDGE

Photo Courtesy Library of Congress

221 MODEL RAILROAD EXHIBIT

If you want to go back in time and take a virtual train ride across the county, visit the Santa Cruz County Railroad Historical Society's (SCCRHS) exhibit at the Santa Cruz County Fairgrounds. Recreating the passenger and commercial railroad era between the 1920s and 1960s with exquisitely detailed dioramas, the society has designed an elaborate HO (1:87) scale layout with 1,000 feet of track that shows the train route through all of Santa Cruz County. The display begins at the Watsonville train yard, runs through tunnels, crosses trestles and passes through the towns of Aptos, Capitola, Santa Cruz and Felton. You will see old Santa Cruz landmarks such as early businesses in Aptos Village, the Seabright Cannery, the Giant Dipper at the Boardwalk, the old Union Ice Plant on Chestnut Street and the Sand Plant in Felton. Outside the exhibit building is an elaborate garden railway display using larger G scale trains and tracks. It features live trees and flowers, seven bridges, three tunnels and various water features. The exhibits can be viewed every September during the Santa Cruz County Fair and on most Monday evenings when the historical society meets. The exhibit building is located on Apple Blossom Lane near the small animal barn and horse arena. When the county fair is closed, use the service entrance past the main entrance on East Lake Avenue.

■ **The Model Railroad exhibit is located at the Santa Cruz County Fairgrounds, 2601 East Lake Avenue, Watsonville.**

Photo Courtesy Robert Ritchey

SCALE MODEL OF THE CAPITOLA TRESTLE CROSSING SOQUEL CREEK

GROVE OF REMEMBRANCE

In 1922, the local American Legion worried that the sacrifice of 14 young Pajaro Valley men who gave their lives in service during World War I would be forgotten. They decided to create a Grove of Remembrance to honor these fallen men. In a public invitation, they wrote that it would not be difficult to raise the needed funds from a few large donors, but "We desire that this memorial shall stand as an expression of Community Sentiment and that EVERY individual in this valley shall feel a personal interest and ownership in this undertaking." Therefore, they asked for contributions not exceeding $10 from any one person. From 1,500 donors, $3,200 was quickly raised, including 5- and 10-cent donations from schoolchildren. A 15-ton boulder was moved to the site and a bronze plaque affixed with the names of the 14 men. A grove of redwood and oak trees was planted and the park was

ready for dedication on July 4, 1923. A short parade took place in Watsonville with Civil War veterans, men of the American Legion and the Boy Scouts, said then to be the "soldiers of yesterday, today and tomorrow."

■ **Today, you can visit this grove and monument at the corner of Freedom Boulevard and Buena Vista Drive, Pajaro Valley.**

THE WORLD WAR I MEMORIAL GROVE OF REMEMBRANCE

CHARLEY PARKHURST GRAVESITE

Charley Darkey Parkhurst (1812–1879) was one of the roughest, toughest stagecoach drivers in the area. He was 5-feet-6-inches tall, wiry and was said to have an unusually high-pitched voice. He didn't talk much about himself, but it was known he was from the East where he had grown up in an orphanage. Charley came to California during the Gold Rush and drove stagecoaches between San Francisco, San Jose, San Juan Bautista, Watsonville and Santa Cruz. Charley had the skills and courage needed to cope with dangerous conditions, including encounters with wild animals and bandits. Charley was known to have shot at least one bandit dead with a single shot. After many years of driving coaches, Charley, suffering from rheumatism and having lost an eye to a horse's kick, retired and ran a stagecoach station.

GRAVESTONE OF CHARLEY PARKHURST, TOUGH
STAGECOACH DRIVER WITH A BIG SECRET

He also worked at lumbering and cattle ranching and then raised chickens near Aptos. He finally died in a small cabin outside Watsonville. As the body was being laid out for burial, an astonishing discovery was made. Charley Parkhurst was, in fact, a woman! Even longtime friends were shocked. Charley was buried in Pioneer Cemetery and in time, the location of the gravesite was forgotten. In 1954, an old cemetery record was discovered that gave the location of Charley's grave and a new marker was erected.

■ **Charley Parkhurst's gravesite is located in Pioneer Cemetery at 66 Marin Street, Watsonville.**

224 GIZDICH RANCH FRUIT JUICER

Gizdich Ranch is a family farm with an apple growing history that began in the early 1930s. Today, more than 15 varieties of apples are grown on the 65-acre farm, as well as strawberries, olallieberries, raspberries, blackberries and boysenberries. Some of the apple varieties, such as Red Delicious and Granny Smith, may be familiar to you. Others such as Black Twig, Pinova or Mutsu, are not well known. If you go to the ranch, be sure to taste samples of the different varieties in the barn. On Saturdays, September through May, you can watch apple or berry juice being made. The crew presses the fruit using a large mechanical juice press connected

APPLE JUICING AT GIZDICH RANCH

to a bottle filler. The day's juicing is often finished by early afternoon, so plan to visit in the morning. Afterward, take a self-guided walk through the apple orchards and berry fields or enjoy a piece of pie at the Bake Shop. When the fruit is in season, the ranch also hosts a you-pick program, a fabulous way for you to enjoy the outdoors and get the freshest fruit grown in the region.

■ **Gizdich Ranch is located at 55 Peckham Road, Watsonville.**

FILLING THE JUICE BOTTLES AT GIZDICH RANCH

MONOLITHS ON BEACH ROAD

If you head from downtown Watsonville, along West Beach Street toward Pajaro Dunes, you will notice three concrete monoliths on your right. The first one sits in front of a farmhouse with a small water tank on top. The next two sit starkly on the edge of Beach Road, towering over acres of farmland. Dated 1912, they look like giant Art Deco chess pieces. They stand about 14 feet high with a 12-foot-wide platform on the top that was probably designed to hold large water towers. Noted Central Coast historian Sandy Lydon speculates that the water towers were used to fill water wagons that would dampen the road dust from the increasing automobile traffic of the time. Whatever their historic purpose, they are an unusual sight. If you are ever visiting Palm or Sunset State Beaches (or just want to take a drive around the scenic farmland area between Watsonville and the bay), these monoliths are worth a closer look.

■ **The monoliths are located on Beach Road, west of Watsonville.**

STANDING BY THE ROAD FOR ABOUT 100 YEARS

THE VIRGIN OF GUADALUPE SHRINE AT PINTO LAKE

Near the water, on the edge of the northern boundary of Pinto Lake in Watsonville, is an elaborate though unofficial community shrine to the Virgin Mary. Hundreds of votive candles, statuary, flowers and colorful banners adorn the area in front of an oak tree where in 1992, the Virgin of Guadalupe appeared to Anita Contreras while she was praying for her children. Now a well-known place of pilgrimage, a series of benches creates a small sanctuary at this lovely spot on the lake. Among the faithful, some are still able to see the foot-high image of the Virgin of Guadalupe in the bark of the tree. She has become known locally, to some, as Our Lady of Watsonville. Along the edge of the lake behind the shrine is a lovely boardwalk with wonderful views of the water, tule plants and wildlife. Pinto Lake is a 92-acre natural spring-fed lake known for trout and bass fishing. There are two parks around the lake. Pinto Lake City Park, at 451 Green Valley Road, has a launch ramp, an RV camping area and many playgrounds. Pinto Lake County Park, where the shrine is located, has nature trails, soccer fields and picnic areas. To get to the park, drive about a mile past the City Park entrance and turn left into the park. The shrine is about a quarter-mile walk down the path along the left side of the soccer field, past the children's playground.

■ **The Virgin of Guadalupe Shrine at Pinto Lake County Park is located at 757 Green Valley Road, Watsonville.**

THE SHRINE IS LOCATED IN A QUIET AREA ON THE EDGE OF PINTO LAKE.

227 WETLANDS OF WATSONVILLE

To discover a hidden treat for hiking, biking or birdwatching right in the middle of the city, head to the wetlands of Watsonville Nature Center. There you will find maps and displays describing one of the most important ecological treasures in the county. Watsonville is home to 800 acres of freshwater marsh, called *sloughs*. The Watsonville wetlands are one of the largest remaining freshwater wetlands along the Central Coast. The soil of the wetlands filters pollution and storm water runoff and helps prevent flooding. Thousands of species of plants and animals live here, including many that are threatened or endangered. As a home to waterfowl, songbirds and raptors, as well as many migrating birds, the wetlands are a great destination for birdwatchers. In 2003, the City of Watsonville established the Wetlands Trails Master Plan with the goal of restoring the wetlands and making them more accessible to the public. You can now wander along miles of easily accessible paved paths with over 30 trail entrances throughout Watsonville. The center, open only on weekends, has animal, plant and cultural history exhibits and a good raised-relief map of the area and its trails. Docents often lead guided trail and birdwatching walks. Bring a pair of binoculars and see a part of Watsonville most people have never seen.

■ **The Watsonville Nature Center is located next to Ramsay Park at 30 Harkins Slough Road, Watsonville.**

THE WETLANDS PROVIDE A HABITAT FOR 26 ENDANGERED ANIMAL AND PLANT SPECIES.

THE EAGLE IN THE TREE

Once you hike up to this rest stop to see the carved wooden eagle in a tree (at the highest point in the Byrne-Milliron Forest Preserve) you will need to take a rest, but you will also be amply rewarded with panoramic views of the magnificent farmlands of the Pajaro Valley. Land Steward Jeff Helmer placed the eagle there more than 25 years ago and has subsequently added many other carvings throughout the preserve. In 1984 the Land Trust of Santa Cruz County, which has been working for over 30 years to protect special properties throughout the county, acquired the 322-acre Byrne Forest, located in the hills above Corralitos. Still a sustainable working timber forest, it is managed for both educational and recreational uses. Crisscrossed with wide dirt trails, the forest is known for its quiet beauty, its excellent birding and for its panoramic views. Many of the trails are steep. (The hike from the trailhead parking area to the Eagle in the Tree rest stop is only about three-quarters of a mile, but climbs almost 700 feet.) The trails are well maintained, however, with wonderful rest areas and little surprises. Signs mark the trails and a good map is available at the trailhead. Adjoining the Byrne Forest is the also-protected 80-acre Ann and James Milliron Forest, known for its old-growth trees including the 1,000-year-old, 250-foot-high "Great White" redwood, named for its south-facing bark that has been bleached white by the sun. While the Byrne-Milliron Forest preserve is accessible to the public, to obtain directions and arrange visits, contact the Land Trust at LandTrustSantaCruz.org and go to their Access and Events section.

THIS EAGLE IS PERCHED 1,600 FEET ABOVE THE PAJARO VALLEY.

■ **The Eagle in the Tree is located in the Byrne-Milliron Forest preserve, off Browns Valley Road, Watsonville.**

APPENDICES

NOTES

We visited and photographed all the sites in this book and most of the descriptions are based on personal observation. Historical data and other facts have primarily been drawn from site brochures or site websites when available. The notes below list outside sources we used, as well as suggestions for further information. We've included some website URLs, but please remember they often can change.

DOWNTOWN SANTA CRUZ & VICINITY

#1: See "Santa Cruz's Town Clock" by Carmen Morones and Rechs Ann Pedersen on the Santa Cruz Public Libraries' website, www.santacruzpl.org/history/articles/42.

#4: See "Notes on the 1906 Aerial Panorama of Santa Cruz by George Lawrence" by Peter Nurkse on the Santa Cruz Public Libraries' website, www.santacruzpl.org/history/articles/182.

#7–8: For more information on war memorials in Santa Cruz see Martha Mendoza's articles in the Santa Cruz Sentinel, "Vets Post Slips Statue onto City Pedestal," 3/9/93, and "Eagle Has Landed," 3/24/93.

#10: For more information on the Del Mar Theatre, see The Sidewalk Companion to Santa Cruz Architecture by John Chase, 1975, p. 130; and the Santa Cruz Sentinel articles, "Del Mar renovation defies national trend" by Dan White, 3/3/2002, and "Del Mar defies national trend, becomes crown of downtown" by Dan White, 11/25/2002.

#11: See "The Octagon" by Margaret Koch, 1978, on the Santa Cruz Public Libraries' website, www.santacruzpl.org/history/articles/39. Read more about The Octagon and other historic Downtown Santa Cruz buildings in the Santa Cruz City Historic Walking Tour brochure entitled "Downtown Now & Then." Find it at the Santa Cruz Planning and Community Development Department, 809 Center Street, Room 206, Santa Cruz, or on the City of Santa Cruz website.

#14: See "Tom Jefferson Scribner, 1899–1982" on the Santa Cruz Public Libraries' website www.santacruzpl.org/history/articles/243.

#16: Crystal Birns, arts program manager for the City of Santa Cruz Economic Development and Redevelopment Agency, provided a wealth of information about the city's mural program, the graphic traffic boxes, and the SculpTOUR installations Downtown. She is an excellent resource for all city-related public art questions.

#17: Thanks to urban forester Leslie Keedy, City of Santa Cruz Parks Division, for information on this Canary Island date palm and other trees in Santa Cruz.

#18: You can read more about architect Lee Dill Esty in "Lee Dill Esty: Architect from Soquel" by Norman Poitevin, included in the book Pathways to the Past: Adventures in Santa Cruz County Architecture, History Journal Number 6, edited by

Joan Gilbert Martin and published in 2009 by the Museum of Art and History at the McPherson Center.

#20: See Wallace Baines' 7/28/2011 article in the *Santa Cruz Sentinel*, "Ann Thiermann's new Downtown mural depicts what Santa Cruz looked and felt like 100 years ago."

#21: You can find more information about architecture on Walnut Avenue in the brochure "Santa Cruz Historic Walking Tour: Walnut Avenue," available in the Santa Cruz City Planning and Community Development Department, 809 Center Street, Room 206, Santa Cruz, or on the City of Santa Cruz website.

#22: Lincoln Court has been awarded a blue plaque, designating it a structure of architectural or historic significance, by the Santa Cruz Museum of Art and History.

#23: For more information on designated heritage trees, see the "City of Santa Cruz Heritage Trees" brochure available at the City of Santa Cruz Parks and Recreation office, 323 Church Street, Santa Cruz.

#25 and #33: For more detailed descriptions of these homes and other historic architecture in Santa Cruz, check out John Chase's *The Sidewalk Companion to Santa Cruz Architecture*, Margaret Koch's *The Walk Around Santa Cruz Book* and the "Santa Cruz Historic Building Survey" series by the City of Santa Cruz.

#26–#32: In addition to the plentiful onsite literature at the historic Santa Cruz Mission complex, be sure to check out the "Santa Cruz Historic Walking Tour: Mission Hill" brochure, available in the City Planning and Community Development Department, 809 Center Street, Room 206, Santa Cruz, or on the City of Santa Cruz website.

#27: Many thanks to Sister Barbara for providing historical newspaper articles concerning the origins of the Holy Cross Church bell.

#34: Thanks to Rachel Anne Goodman, former executive director of the Tannery Arts Center, for sharing her knowledge and enthusiasm about the center.

#35: See Garth Merrill's 12/9/1998 article in the *Scotts Valley Banner*: "SV Scout gives face lift to totem pole."

#37: Evergreen Cemetery is maintained by the Santa Cruz Museum of Art and History at the McPherson Center. Contact the museum or see their website at www.santacruzmah.org for information about guided tours of Evergreen Cemetery throughout the year.

#38: See "The Pogonip" by Ross Eric Gibson on the Santa Cruz Public Libraries' website, www.santacruzpl.org/history/articles/27. See also "Pogonip gets a makeover," *Santa Cruz Sentinel*, Genevieve Bookwalter, *Sentinel* staff writer, 03/16/2009.

#39: Janet and Randy Krassow's informative historical guide and walking map to the cemetery called "A Walk Through Time," can be found online at the Santa Cruz Public Libraries' website, www.santacruzpl.org/history/articles/429. Copies may also be available at the Memorial Park office.

#44: Thanks to Crystal Birns, arts program manager for the City of Santa Cruz Economic Development and Redevelopment Agency for providing information about Riverbend Plaza Park.

#47: See the series of articles on the Carmelita Cottages by Rick Hyman, available on the Santa Cruz Public Libraries' website, www.santacruzpl.org/history/articles/597.

#48: You can find more information about architecture on Beach Hill in the brochure "Santa Cruz Historic Walking Tour: Beach Hill," available in the City Planning and Community Development Department, 809 Center Street, Room 206, Santa Cruz, or on the city's website.

#49: For additional interesting facts about the Giant Dipper and other roller coasters around the country, check out http://coaster-net.com.

#52: The poem excerpt is reprinted with kind permission from Alan Counihan, author and sculptor of In the Tides of Time.

#55: Information taken from "The West Cliff Inn of Santa Cruz, CA…A Little History" by Shanna McCord, available at the West Cliff Inn. Many thanks also to Amy Dunning, archivist and research librarian at the Museum of Art and History at the McPherson Center for her help in researching the Lynch House and for sourcing many other important historical facts helpful to the writing of this book. The quote used here is from Santa Cruz County, California: Illustrations Descriptive of its Scenery, Fine Residences, Public Buildings, Manufactories, Hotels, Farm Scenes, Business Houses, Schools, Churches, Mines, Mills, etc., with Historical Sketch of the County, Wallace W. Elliott & Co., San Francisco, 1879.

WESTSIDE SANTA CRUZ

#62: See Joel Hersch's 5/25/2011 article in the Santa Cruz Sentinel, "Museum Surfs In to 25 Years."

#69: For more detailed information about "Ms. Blue," visit the Seymour Marine Discover Center website, which includes the text of Dave Casper's keynote address at the Blue Whale dedication in 2001, http://seymourcenter.ucsc.edu/press_releases/Blue_Whale_Skeleton.pdf.

#70: Go to the Channel Islands Marine Sanctuary Shipwreck Database for more information about the wreck of the La Feliz, http://channelislands.noaa.gov/shipwreck/dbase/mbnms/lafeliz.html.

#71: See UCSC science writer Tim Steven's 7/23/2004 article, "New elephant seal sculpture at the Seymour Marine Discovery Center honors Long Marine Lab volunteers," http://news.ucsc.edu/2004/07/530.html.

#72: See "Court of the Mysteries; Brothers Build Unusual Old Yoga Temple" by Ross Eric Gibson on the Santa Cruz Public Libraries' website, www.santacruzpl.org/history/articles/27. Also, for fun reading, find "If You Can't Take the Heat – Get Out of the Kitchen Brothers," by The Kitchen Sisters, Davia Nelson and Nikki Silva, at www.npr.org/programs/lnfsound/scrapbook/kitchensisters.html. Finally, check out "What the Heck Is That? A Yogi Temple? Or?" by Sandy Lydon at www.sandylydon.com/sec.html.

#75: For more information on the Home of Peace Cemetery and Jewish history of Santa Cruz, see the Temple Beth El website at www.tbeaptos.org. See also Ross Gibson's article "Jewish Pioneers Played a Big Role in Santa Cruz," on the Santa Cruz Public Libraries' website, www.santacruzpl.org/history/articles/121.

#76: Historical information about Antonelli Pond is from *Santa Cruz County Place Names*, by Donald T. Clark, 1986.

UC SANTA CRUZ

#78–80: The Friends of the Cowell Lime Works work to restore and preserve the old limekilns and historic buildings of the Cowell Lime Works Historic District. You can visit their website at http://limeworks.ucsc.edu to read more about the Cowell Lime Works Historic District and to access a self-guided walking tour of the District adapted from the book *Lime Kiln Legacies* by Frank Perry, Robert W. Piwarzyk, Michael D. Luther, Alverda Orlando, Allan Molho and Sierra L. Perry, published by The Museum of Art and History.

#81–82: The UCSC Center for Agroecology & Sustainable Food Systems has an extensive and informative website about its activities, many of which are available to the public. See http://casfs.ucsc.edu.

#84: Special thanks to Chris Lay, museum scientist and curator for the National History Collections. The museum website is very informative and includes a wonderful section on the Natural History of the UCSC campus. See http://mnhc.ucsc.edu.

#88: For more information see "Porter Totem Pole" by Jeff Arnett in his wonderful book, *An Unnatural History of UCSC*.

#92: Detailed information about the UCSC Arboretum, its collection and activities can be found online at http://arboretum.ucsc.edu.

SAN LORENZO VALLEY & SCOTTS VALLEY

#94–96: The California Powder Works & San Lorenzo Paper Mill Self-Guided Tour by Barry Brown, 2008, is a comprehensive history of Paradise Park and is available at the Park office. See also the Santa Cruz Public Libraries' website at www.santacruzpl. org/history/authors/80 for more articles on the California Powder Works and the San Lorenzo Paper Mill by Barry Brown. Thanks to Cyndy Crogan, manager at Paradise Park, for sharing her knowledge and enthusiasm for her community.

#99: For more on the Felton Covered Bridge and other covered bridges in Santa Cruz County, see "Covered Bridges" by John V. Young on the Santa Cruz Public Libraries' website, www.santacruzpl.org/history/articles/4; and "Bridges Span Santa Cruz's Past: From Felton's Covered Redwood Span to West Cliff Drive's Iron Landmark," by Ross Eric Gibson, www.santacruzpl.org/history/articles/19.

#106: For a complete history of Fall Creek, see the Mountain Parks Foundation website at http://mountainparks.org/fall-creek.

#108: Many thanks to Frances Taber for sharing her memories of her uncle, Nick Belardi, and the Felton of her childhood.

#109: See "Howden's Castle" by Margaret Koch on the Santa Cruz Public Libraries' website, www.santacruzpl.org/history/articles/30.

#110: See the Santa Cruz Mountain Arts Center website for more information on the center and its activities, www.mountainartcenter.org.

#113: Thanks to Alba Schoolhouse neighbor Anne Brown for generously sharing her knowledge and enthusiasm for this historic building.

#114–115: Thanks to Lisa Robinson, collections manager at the San Lorenzo Valley Museum, for sharing stories of San Lorenzo Valley history and providing background on the history of the *Mountain Echo*.

#117: Goat Rock is just one of thousands of entries in Donald Thomas Clark's seminal geographical dictionary, *Santa Cruz County Place Names*, published by Kestrel Press.

#118: Many thanks to Eric Taylor of the Scotts Valley Historical Society for providing information on the Scott House, including his article "Hiram Daniel Scott, Scotts Valley's Namesake," which appeared in the *Scotts Valley Times*, January 2003, and also for sharing his vast knowledge and personal memories of the history of Scotts Valley.

#120: For additional information see "What was SV area like 10,000 years ago?" from Lisa Levinson's *Scotts Valley Banner* article of August 15, 1990, posted on the Scotts Valley Chamber of Commerce website. For other interesting sites in Scotts Valley, see "Scotts Valley Area Curiosities" by Marion Dale Pokriots on the

Santa Cruz Public Libraries' local history website, www.santacruzpl.org/history/articles/186.

#124: See the display of the Tree Circus in the "Where the Redwoods Meet the Sea: A History of Santa Cruz and its People" exhibit at the Santa Cruz Museum of Art and History in Santa Cruz.

#125: See the following *Santa Cruz Sentinel* articles: "City Sign Law Effective at Stroke of Midnight" by John Elliott 12/11/66; "Billboards' extinction: sign of times" by Joan Raymond 8/12/86; and "Ordinary laws of billboards are no longer suspended" by Kathy Kreiger 9/29/95.

THE NORTH COAST

#127–131: Special thanks to Stephan Bianchi, Wilder Ranch docent, for sharing his detailed knowledge of Wilder Ranch.

#132: See the discussion of the Ocean Shore Electric Railway and the Ocean Shore Stream Tunnels within the "Coast Dairies Property: A Land Use History" article on the Santa Cruz County History section of the Santa Cruz Public Libraries' website. Renowned local historian Sandy Lydon also has a comprehensive article on the ramparts and tunnels in the Secret History section of his website, www.SandyLydon.com.

#133–134: Thanks to Alverda Orlando for sharing her memories and knowledge of Davenport history. For more information on the history of Davenport see "Early History of Davenport" by Alverda Orlando on the Santa Cruz Public Libraries' website, www.santacruzpl.org/history/articles/394. See also *Santa Cruz County Parade of the Past*, Margaret Koch, 1973, for more information on the Davenport Jail.

#135: Special thanks to Ed Carnegie, director of the Swanton Pacific Railroad, for information about access to the property.

#137–138: Among many other fascinating stories, the wonderful book *Memories of the Mountain* by The Ladies of Bonny Doon Club includes insightful chapters on "The Lost Weekend" (by Richard Tiffin and Pat Pfremmer) and "The Bonny Doon Ecological Reserve" (by Barbara Louv).

EASTSIDE SANTA CRUZ

#140: See Brian Seals' 12/1/2001 *Santa Cruz Sentinel* article "New Lighthouse topped off," and the websites www.LighthouseFriends.com and www.BeachCalifornia.com.

#145: Special thanks to Ann Thiermann, who graciously shared stories of this mural and her other Ohlone Indian mural projects.

#147: See the California Department of Fish and Wildlife Report: "Verified Mountain Lion Attacks on Humans in California (1890 through 2013)," and also check out their "Commonly Asked Questions" for more information and safety tips. See www.dfg.ca.gov/wildlife/lion/attacks.html.

#151: You can find more information about the historic homes on Ocean View Avenue in the guide "Santa Cruz Historic Walking Tour: Ocean View Avenue," available in the Santa Cruz City Planning and Community Development Department, 809 Center Street, Room 206, Santa Cruz, or on the City of Santa Cruz website.

#152: For a detailed explanation of the building of the skate park read "Catching the Concrete Wave: Skate Park at Mike Fox Park, Santa Cruz, Calif.," by Amy Johnson, in the May 2007 issue of *Concrete Décor*. Three different sources gave three different sizes for the full pipe (16, 17, and 18 feet). We went with the Friends of Parks and Recreation's 17-foot figure.

#160: See Liz Kersjes' 11/5/2009 *Santa Cruz Sentinel* article "Live Oak Elementary welcomes home historic bell," and Melissa Weaver's 11/12/2009 posting on the Santa Cruz Museum of Art and History's research forum website.

MID-COUNTY: CAPITOLA, SOQUEL, APTOS, RIO DEL MAR

#162–163: For a self-guided walking tour of Capitola, see museum director Carolyn Swift's "Capitola Walking Tour" guide, available at the Capitola Historical Museum, and online at the museum's website.

#164: Information and quotes about the Capitola tiki are from various articles and editorials appearing in the *Santa Cruz Sentinel* from 10/15/2008 to 5/06/2009.

#165: The Capitola Art & Cultural Commission has prepared a complete pictorial record of every one of the 1,200 seawall tiles produced by Capitola residents, along with short stories from the participants. Contact the commission for more information.

#170: Information is from various articles in the *Santa Cruz Sentinel* including "Rispin Mansion Looking Better After $648,850 Makeover," by Jondi Gumz, 2/8/2012.

#172: For more information on Capitola's Riverview Historic District, see "Old Riverview Avenue Historic District of Capitola" on the Santa Cruz Public Libraries' website, www.santacruzpl.org/history/articles/399.

#176: For a definitive history of the Cement Ship, see David Heron's *Forever Facing South, The Story of the S.S.* Palo Alto, published in 2002 by Otter B. Books. The delightful website www.concreteships.org is also a great place for information about the Palo Alto and other concrete ships from WWI and WWII.

#177: See Perry, Frank A. 1988. *Fossil Invertebrates and Geology of the Marine Cliffs at Capitola, California*, Santa Cruz Museum Association.

#179: For much more information about Land of the Medicine Buddha's grounds and activities, see the retreat's website at www.medicinebuddha.org.

#181 and #187: Historical information about Redwood Village and the Bay View Hotel was provided by John Hibble, curator of the Aptos History Museum.

#186: See James R. Spurgeon's 6/10/1979 *Santa Cruz Sentinel* article "Plans Readied for Monument to Pioneer Aviator," and check out www.flyingmachines. org for photographs of John Montgomery and schematics of many of his gliders.

#191: The historical information about Valencia Hall and Valencia Post Office is from a speech by John Hibble at the reopening of Valencia Hall.

#194: For more information about the epicenter, see the U.S. Geological Survey article "Forest of Nisene Marks State Park: Epicenter of the 1989 Loma Prieta Earthquake" on the USGS website. For a great book on the history and trails of the park see Jeff Thomson's book *Explore the Forest of Nisene Marks State Park*, published by Walkabout Publications.

SOUTH COUNTY: WATSONVILLE & LA SELVA BEACH

#195: For a walking guide to all of Watsonville's downtown apple label murals including a map of their locations, see http://growinwatsonville.com/living-in-watsonville/historic-downtown/murals.

#196–198: Information about the history and development of La Selva is from Robin S. Batchelor's delightful 24-page booklet, "La Selva Beach," published in February 1984. It is available through the Santa Cruz Public Libraries.

#199: Historical information from "Historic Gas Station," prepared for the Museum of Art and History 2010 Blue Plaque Awards.

#200: For a self-guided tour of downtown Watsonville—including St. Patrick's Church, the Plaza and many of the historic buildings on Main Street—download the "Walking and Driving Tour of Historic Main Street" at cityofwatsonville.org/download/Visitors/Historic_Walking_Tour.pdf.

#201–202: For a concise history of Watsonville Plaza, see Betty Lewis's 3/21/2007 *Register-Pajaronian* article "Beautifying the Public Square: A Lasting Effort."

#203–204: Geoffrey Dunn, who with Sandy Lydon co-authored the feasibility study that established the CAWHC, wrote a moving opinion piece on the project for the *Register-Pajaronian* on 12/20/2008 entitled "Why are there artichokes in the Watsonville Public Library Mural?" This article is worth seeking out.

#208: Heartfelt thanks to retired Fire Chief Gene Friend for his personal tour of the Fire Museum, and for sharing his memories and vast knowledge of the museum and the history of firefighting in Watsonville.

#209 and #211: See Amanda Schoenberg's 3/27/2007 *Register-Pajaronian* article "Tank House"; and Jane Borg's 2007 "Historic Bockius-Orr House and Garden" description on the Pajaro Valley Historical Association website.

#210: For more about the history of square grand pianos, see the article "What Is a Square Grand Piano?" at www.AntiquePianoShop.com.

#214: See *Victorian Houses of Watsonville* by Watsonville historian Betty Lewis, 1974 (revised in 1981), Pajaro Valley Historical Association. For more history on Watsonville, Betty Lewis has written several fine books and articles about the history of the city.

#215: Thanks to Father Al Mengon of Our Lady Help of Christians Valley Church for generously loaning a briefcase full of archival materials about the history of the Valley Church.

#216–219: For more information about the Agricultural History Project, visit their website at www.aghistoryproject.org.

#220: Many thanks to Loretta Estrada of the Rodgers House Committee for sharing her knowledge and enthusiasm about the Rodgers House and for hosting private access to the house for this book.

#221: For more information about model railroading, the difference between HO scale and G scale, and to find out how to join the Santa Cruz County Railroad Historical Society, go to www.trainweb.org/sccrhs.

#222–223: Many thanks to the wonderful Jane Borg of the Pajaro Valley Historical Association for sharing her knowledge of the Pioneer Cemetery, and for her help in sourcing archival materials on Charlie Parkhurst's gravesite and the World War I Memorial.

#227: See Dan Haifley's 1/9/2010 Our Ocean Backyard column in the *Santa Cruz Sentinel* entitled "By the Waterside" for more information about the sloughs of Watsonville.

#228: Many thanks to Byrne Forest caretaker Jeff Helmer for his work in helping preserve and maintain this beautiful forest.

SANTA CRUZ COUNTY MUSEUMS & ART GALLERIES

The Santa Cruz County Museum Partnership has published a comprehensive brochure and online listing of local museums and art galleries, and we have reproduced the names, addresses, and contact information for each below. We also added the California Agricultural Workers' History Center. Interesting objects that can be found in each of these museums and galleries are described throughout this book. Their description number(s) are noted in bold. For complete information about the museums and galleries, including hours, prices and parking, go to www.SantaCruzCountyMuseums.org or contact the individual sites directly. Please note that telephone numbers and website URLs are subject to change.

HISTORY MUSEUMS

Agricultural History Project (See #216–219)
2601 East Lake Avenue, Watsonville, CA 95076
831-724-5898
www.aghistoryproject.org

Aptos History Museum (See #184–185)
7605-B Old Dominion Court, Aptos, CA 95003
831-688-1467
www.aptoshistory.org

California Agricultural Workers' History Center (See #203–204)
Watsonville Public Library
275 Main Street, 2nd Floor, Watsonville, CA 95076
831-768-3400
www.cityofwatsonville.org/public-library/research-center/california-agricultural-workers-history-center

Capitola Historical Museum (See #162–163)
410 Capitola Avenue, Capitola, CA 95010
831-464-0322
www.capitolamuseum.org

Cowell Lime Works (See #78–80)
UCSC Historic District
1156 High Street, Santa Cruz, CA 95064
831-459-1254
http://limeworks.ucsc.edu

Pacific Migrations Visitor Center (See #178)
New Brighton State Beach
1500 Park Avenue, Capitola, CA 95010
831-464-5620
www.thatsmypark.org/cp-parks-beaches/new-brighton-state-beach

Santa Cruz Mission State Historic Park (See #26–30)
144 School Street, Santa Cruz, CA 95060
831-425-5849
www.thatsmypark.org/cp-parks-beaches/santa-cruz-mission-state-historic-park

Wilder Ranch State Park (See #127–131)
1401 Old Coast Road, Santa Cruz, CA 95060
831-426-0505
www.thatsmypark.org/cp-parks-beaches/wilder-ranch-state-park

Museum of Art and History (See #13)
McPherson Center
705 Front Street, Santa Cruz, CA 95060
831-429-1964
www.santacruzmah.org

Pajaro Valley Historical Association (See #209–211)
332 East Beach Street, Watsonville, CA 95076
831-722-0305
www.pajarovalleyhistory.org

Quail Hollow Ranch County Park (See #107)
800 Quail Hollow Road, Felton, CA 95018
831-335-9348
www.scparks.com/quail_hollow.html

Rodgers House (See #220)
Santa Cruz County Fairgrounds
2601 East Lake Avenue, Watsonville, CA 95076
831-724-5671
www.santacruzcountyfair.com/rodgers-house

San Lorenzo Valley Museum (See #114–115)
12547 Highway 9, Boulder Creek, CA 95006
831-338-8382
www.slvmuseum.com

Santa Cruz Beach Boardwalk Historium (See #51)
400 Beach Street, Santa Cruz, CA 95060
831-423-5590

Santa Cruz Surfing Museum (See #61–62)
Mark Abbot Memorial Lighthouse
701 West Cliff Drive, Santa Cruz, CA 95060
831-420-6289
www.santacruzsurfingmuseum.org

Soquel Pioneer and Historical Association
Porter Memorial Public Library
3050 Porter Street, Soquel, CA 95073
831-475-3326
www.soquelpioneers.com

Watsonville Fire Department Museum (See #208)
105 Second Street, Watsonville, CA 95076
831-768-3202

NATURAL HISTORY MUSEUMS

Big Basin Redwoods State Park Nature Museum (See #93)
21600 Big Basin Way, Boulder Creek, CA 95006
831-338-8883
www.bigbasin.org

Monterey Bay Sanctuary Exploration Center (See #57)
35 Pacific Avenue, Santa Cruz, CA 95060
831-421-9993
www.montereybay.noaa.gov/vc/sec

Natural Bridges State Beach Visitor Center (See #67–68)
2531 West Cliff Drive, Santa Cruz, CA 95060
831-423-4609
www.thatsmypark.org/cp-parks-beaches/natural-bridges-state-park

Rancho del Oso (See #136)
Nature and History Center
3600 Highway 1, Davenport, CA 95017
831-427-2288
www.ranchodeloso.org

Seacliff State Beach Visitor Center (See #176)
201 State Park Drive, Aptos, CA 95003
831-685-6444
www.thatsmypark.org/cp-parks-beaches/seacliff-state-beach

Henry Cowell Redwoods State Park Visitor Center (See #101–104)
525 North Big Trees Park Road, Felton, CA 95018
831-335-8418
www.thatsmypark.org/cp-parks-beaches/henry-cowell-redwoods-state-park

Santa Cruz Museum of Natural History (See #145–148)
1305 East Cliff Drive, Santa Cruz, CA 95062
831-420-6115
www.santacruzmuseums.org

Seymour Center at Long Marine Lab (See #69–71)
100 Shaffer Road, Santa Cruz, CA 95060
831-459-3800
http://seymourcenter.ucsc.edu

Watsonville Nature Center (See #227)
30 Harkins Slough Road, Watsonville, CA 95076
831-768-1622
http://cityofwatsonville.org/public-works-utilities/conservation_outreach_and_
education_program/nature-center

ART GALLERIES

Cabrillo College Library (See #182)
Robert E. Swenson Library, Room 1002
6500 Soquel Drive, Aptos, CA 95003
831-479-6308
www.cabrillo.edu/services/artgallery

Eloise Pickard Smith Art Gallery (See #86)
Cowell College, UCSC
1156 High Street, Santa Cruz, CA 95064
831-459-2953
http://cowell.ucsc.edu/smith-gallery

Mary Porter Sesnon Art Gallery (See #87)
Porter College, UCSC
1156 High Street, Santa Cruz, CA 95064
831-459-3606
http://art.ucsc.edu/galleries/sesnon/current

Museum of Art and History (See #13)
McPherson Center
705 Front Street, Santa Cruz, CA 95060
831-429-1964
www.santacruzmah.org

Pajaro Valley Arts Council Gallery (See #212–213)
37 Sudden Street, Watsonville, CA 95076
831-722-3062
www.pajarovalleyartscouncil.org

Sierra Azul Nursery and Gardens (See #213)
2660 East Lake Avenue, Watsonville, CA 95076
831-763-0939
www.sierraazul.com

Santa Cruz Art League (See #153)
526 Broadway, Santa Cruz, CA 95060
831-426-5787
www.scal.org

Santa Cruz Mountains Art Center (See #110)
9341 Mill Street, Ben Lomond, CA 95005
831-336-3513
www.mountainartcenter.org

Santa Cruz County Arts Commission (See #12)
Santa Cruz County Government Center Exhibitions
1701 Ocean Street, Santa Cruz, CA 95060
831-454-7901 or 831-454-2000
www.scparks.com/public_art.html

Scotts Valley Artisans
230D Mt. Hermon Road, Scotts Valley, CA 95066
831-439-9094
www.scottsvalleyartisans.com

Tannery Arts Center (See #34)
1050 River Street, Santa Cruz, CA 95060
831-621-6226
www.tanneryartscenter.org

SELECTED BIBLIOGRAPHY OF BOOKS ABOUT SANTA CRUZ COUNTY

There are many wonderful books on Santa Cruz County. Some of our favorites are listed below. All are available at the Santa Cruz Public Library, and most are available at the Watsonville Public Library.

Arnett, Jeff, ed. *An Unnatural History of UCSC*. Santa Cruz: Bay Tree Bookstore, 2008.

Beal, Richard A. *Highway 17: The Road to Santa Cruz*. Aptos, CA: The Pacific Group, 1991.

Brown, Eileen, and Steven Bignell. *Santa Cruz: A Guide for Runners, Joggers and Serious Walkers*. Santa Cruz, CA: Journeyworks Publishing, 2005.

Chase, John Leighton. *The Sidewalk Companion to Santa Cruz Architecture*. Santa Cruz, CA: The Museum of Art and History, Third Edition 2005. First published 1975 by John Chase.

Clark, Donald Thomas. *Santa Cruz County Place Names: A Geographical Dictionary*. Kestrel Press, rev. ed., 2008. First published 1986 by the Santa Cruz Historical Society.

Dunn, Geoffrey F. *Santa Cruz Is in the Heart*. Capitola, CA: Capitola Book Company, 1995.

Heron, David. *Forever Facing South: The Story of the S.S.Palo Alto "The Old Cement Ship" of Seacliff Beach*. Santa Cruz, CA: Otter B. Books, 1991.

Koch, Margaret. *Santa Cruz County—Parade of the Past*. Santa Cruz, CA: Western Tanager Press/Valley Publishers, 1973.

Lewis, Betty. *Watsonville, Memories That Linger, Volume 1*. Santa Cruz, CA: Valley Publishers, 1976.

Lewis, Betty. *Watsonville, Memories That Linger, Volume 2*. Santa Cruz, CA: Valley Publishers, 1980.

Lydon, Sandy. *Chinese Gold: The Chinese in the Monterey Bay Region*. Capitola, CA: Capitola Book Company, 1985.

McCarthy, Nancy. *Where Grizzlies Roamed the Canyons*. Palo Alto, CA: Garden Court Press, 1994.

Perry, Frank A. *Lighthouse Point Illuminating Santa Cruz*. Santa Cruz, CA: Otter B Books, 2002.

Rowland, Leon. *Santa Cruz, The Early Years*. Santa Cruz, CA: Paper Vision Press, 1980.

Thomson, Jeff. *Explore…The Forest of Nisene Marks State Park*. Soquel, CA: Walkabout Publications, 2001.

In addition to the above books, the City of Santa Cruz Department of Planning and Community Development has also commissioned the following surveys of historical properties in the City of Santa Cruz:

Historic Context Statement for the City of Santa Cruz. Susan Lehmann, October 20, 2000.

Santa Cruz Historic Building Survey, Volume I. Charles Hall Page & Associates, Inc., San Francisco, CA. 1976.

Santa Cruz Historic Building Survey, Volume II. John Chase and Daryl Allen, Santa Cruz, CA. May 1989.

SUBJECT INDEX

ABOUT THE AUTHORS

SUSAN BRUIJNES

Susan's first memory of Santa Cruz is the time she sprained her finger trying to walk through the spinning barrel in the Boardwalk's Fun House when she was 7 years old. That finger is still crooked. As a child, she marveled at seeing Santa Claus and his elves in August at long-gone Santa's Village in Scotts Valley; and like many others, she spent lazy summers at camps in the Santa Cruz Mountains. Finally, in 1997, she made Santa Cruz her home and really began to discover how much there is to see and learn in this diverse county. Even after working on this book, Susan has a lot of exploring left to do.

STEVEN BIGNELL

Steven is old enough to remember when the slide at the Boardwalk's saltwater Plunge was as scary as the Giant Dipper, when Seabright Beach had a castle, and the dinosaurs of Scotts Valley's Lost World greeted cars driving over Highway 17. Although he came to Santa Cruz often as a kid, Steven didn't move here until 1968 as an early UCSC student. After 45 years he thought he knew Santa Cruz County really well (especially being married to a third-generation Watsonville native), but working on this book showed him that no matter how long you've lived here there is always something new to discover.

Steven is publisher at Journeyworks Publishing and also co-wrote *Santa Cruz: A Guide for Runners, Joggers and Serious Walkers*.